Strength
Like an Eagle
(A Renewed You)

Jimmy R. Stevens

authorHOUSE®

AuthorHouse™
1663 Liberty Drive
Bloomington, IN 47403
www.authorhouse.com
Phone: 1-800-839-8640

Published by AuthorHouse 11/30/2012

ISBN: 978-1-4772-8131-4 (e)
ISBN: 978-1-4772-8132-1 (sc)
ISBN: 978-1-4772-8133-8 (hc)

Library of Congress Control Number: 2012919468

Welcome

I was present at an old fashion revival conference called the "Love Conference" when the guest speaker began to elaborate on the eagle. The insights and revelation that he brought forth that night touched on a reality that too many people are facing. Too many people are living beyond their God given potential and purpose. Too many people are trapped in a mind-set of poverty, and pitifulness. Too many people are walking in the dirt of mediocrity and have succumbed to an existence of failure and frustration. Too many people have bought into the lies of the Enemy and allowed the hounds of hell to intimidate them with the paralyzing emotions of fear, distrust and envy.

Yet you have been created to be and do so much more. You have been created with an extraordinary brain to be creative and a heart to feel the beat of possibilities. You have been downloaded with talents, a unique personality, and a divinely designed temperament. Your DNA code is filled with the potential to think great thoughts and accomplish great deeds. You have a God of infinite wisdom and unsearchable knowledge. You have been given a measure of faith to allow you to connect to the supernatural and the eternal. You have been shaped and formed to be like an eagle. You have been created to soar to the heights of your dreams, visions and your assignment on this planet. Yet God has created you with a void that can be only filled by Him.

I was moved to preach a series of sermons on the eagle that richly blessed my congregation. I sincerely believe that you need to be blessed as well from these life changing words. These materials are taken at large from that series and I know that you will richly be challenged and changed as you work through these materials and listen to the audio messages as well. This exciting study entitled "God Will Renew Your Strength" is taken from Isaiah 40:28-31. You are beginning a journey of spiritual empowerment as you discover who God really created you to be. Also you will begin with new insight to work through the past season of your life and begin to put to rest past pain, disappointments, unrealistic expectations, unresolved issues, unhealed hurts and struggles. You will be strengthen in this present season and God moment in your life where God is producing change and growth.

Finally, I believe that you will be renewed and refreshed for the faith journey ahead. We ask that you make the commitment to start and complete this educational and spiritual journey and see the Hand of God move in your life. You have been created to soar like an eagle.

Jimmy R. Stevens

Table of Contents

"God Will Renew Your Strength Like an Eagle"
Bible Study – Isaiah 40:28-31

Chapter 1 –
You Can Have an Eagle Mentality

The Almighty God in His word uses metaphors, symbols, and word pictures to describe us as believers! One of the word pictures that God uses in His word is that He describes you as an "eagle"! An eagle is a majestic bird. Perhaps God's greatest bird! Eagles are members of the bird family Accipitridae. Eagles are large, powerful built, with a heavy head and beak.

For thousands of years the eagle has been respected for its grandeur. There is something inspiring about its impressive grace in flight, its great wingspan, its powerful claw. It glides effortlessly at breathtaking altitudes, seemingly unaffected by the turbulent winds that whip across and between mountain crevices. Eagles do not travel in flocks nor do they conduct themselves irresponsibly. Strong of heart and solitary, they represent qualities we admire. The eagle mates for life and returns to the same nest each year, making necessary repairs and additions. He takes an active role in providing for his family, protecting it from approaching dangers, and teaching little eaglets to fly. Responsibility, liberty, beauty, stability, and other admirable traits seen woven into the eagle's makeup, and such qualities cause me to agree with Solomon that "the way of an eagle in the sky" is nothing short of "wonderful" (Proverbs 30:18-19).[1] The eagle is so awesome that there are seven characteristics of his uniqueness.

Seven Unique Characteristics of the Eagle

- Fearless – The eagle has absolutely no fear of its prey, no matter what size. II Timothy 1:7 "God has not given us a spirit of fear; but of power and of love and of a sound mind".

- Tenacious – The eagle looks and flies not from the storm but flies into the storm. The eagle spreads its wings and mounts upon the powerful winds, soaring to great heights by using the wind of the storm to lift it higher!

- Nurturing – There is no member of the bird family that is so gentle and attentive to their young as the eagle. At the right time, the mother eagle begins to teach her eaglets how to fly. She gathers an eaglet on her back, and spreading her wings, flies high. Suddenly she swoops out from under the eaglet and allows it to fall. As it fails, it gradually learns what its wings are for until the mother catches it once again. The process is repeated. If the young is slow to learn or cowardly, she returns it to the nest, and begins to tear it apart, until there is nothing left for the eaglet to cling to. Then she nudges him off the cliff.

- High-Flier – The eagle can fly at an altitude of 10,000 feet, but they are able to swiftly land to the ground. The descending glide of an eagle can be anywhere from 50-75 mph. Higher than any other bird at a speed of 150 miles per hour.

- Eagles Never Eat Dead Meat- You will never see an eagle eating meat that it did not kill. An eagle is not a scavenger. It hunts for and kills its own food. It hunts for its prey while it's warm and alive.

- Vitality – An eagle is full of life and has the power to endure. By the time the eagle reaches about 30 years of age, life gets hard. Its physical condition has deteriorated to the point where survival is difficult. But the eagle retreats to a mountaintop and over a five month period goes through a metamorphosis, allowing the eagle to live another 30-40 years.

- Vision–The eagle has keen vision. He has eight times as many visual cells per cubic centimeter than does a human. This translates into rather astounding abilities. The eagle can spot an object the size of a dime moving through six-inch grass. The same creature can see three-inch fish jumping in a lake five miles away. He can spot another eagle "50 miles" away and a rabbit in a bush 3 to 5 miles. Eagle like people can envision what most would miss.

God created you and I to be like the eagle! Not like

chickens, pigeons or peacocks! But like eagles! In Isaiah chapter forty, the children of Israel was in captivity! They were going through hard and difficult times but God wanted them to know that they had to have an eagle mentality to make it. An eagle experiences at least three seasons in life: the discovery and growth season, the molting season and the renewal season. In Isaiah 40:28 there are two questions that the prophet asks. The two questions are (Have you not known? and have you not seen?). God wants you to discover who He is! God constantly allows you and I to **"Discover and Grow "**!

> **Have you not known? Have you not heard? The Lord is the everlasting God, the Creator of the ends of the earth. He will not grow tired or weary, and his understanding no one can fathom. (Isaiah 40:28) NIV**

The Eagle Stirs the Nest

It's interesting how a little eaglet discovers how to fly. The mother eaglet builds a nest up into the mountains or highest point of a tree! She carefully or meticulously pads the nest with twigs, branches and then soft grass and makes the nest as comfortable for the little eaglet as she can. But then when she discerns that it is time for the little eaglets to fly according to Deuteronomy 32:11,**"The eagle stirs up its nest**."

The mother eagle begins to pull out the soft stuff in the nest so that the nest becomes uncomfortable and the little twigs and branches begin to stick the eaglet to the point where the little eaglet will want to discover another environment. She spreads her wings and allows the eaglet to ride on her wings and takes the little eaglet up and drops him. The little eaglet falls and flutters and then began to flap his wings and discover who he really is. The little eaglet discovers that he has been created to fly! The little eaglet spreads its wings and soars through the sky.

> **Deuteronomy 32:11, "As an eagle stirs up its nest, hovers over its young, spreading out its wings, taking them up, carrying them on its wings."**

Developing an Eagle Mentality

Our times demand that believers have an eagle mentality. Remember that the eagle is fearless, tenacious, nurturing, high-flier, full of vitality and visionary. Retraining and reprogramming your mind is essential to developing an eagle mentality. Getting a new mental picture is hard work. This thought life is not automatically changed. The change in our thinking is a product of effective action. The bible calls this process a metamorphosis!

> **"I beseech you therefore, brethren, by the mercies of God, that ye present your bodies a living sacrifice, holy, acceptable unto God, which is your reasonable service. And be not conformed to this world: but be ye transformed by the renewing of your mind, that ye may prove what is that good, and acceptable, and perfect will of God." Romans 12:1-2**

> **"And be renewed in the spirit of your mind." Ephesians 4:23**

Sources of Your Thinking

Incorrect thinking will cripple your decision-making; it will retard your faith and keep you from overcoming life's challenges. Our belief system or value system has been shaped from **four sources**. The four factors that work to shape our value system and belief system which become the basis for our decision making are social environment; credible authority figures in our lives; repetitious information; and personal experiences. First, our **social environment** helps shape what we believe about the world around us. The social environment imposes certain truths about life that affect the development of our value system. Secondly, the **authority figures** in our lives teach us certain things about life and living that become a part of our value system. These authority figures such as our parents, relatives, teachers and ministers, those whom we respect and listen to, affect how to choose to believe about life. Thirdly, our minds are designed to accept **information** that is fed to it on a consistent, repetitious basis. Whatever I hear over and over again eventually makes its way into my thought pattern. Finally, our belief system is shaped by our **personal experiences** that we have. The most potent impact on the way we think is what we have experienced.[2]

I'm sure it comes as no surprise to most of us that we act out precisely what we take in. In other words, we become what we think. Long before that familiar line found its way into Psychology 101 and hyped-up sales meetings, the Bible included it in one of its ancient scrolls; it just said it in a little different way, "For as he thinks within himself, so he is" (Proverbs 23:7). The secret of living a life of excellence is merely a matter of thinking thoughts of excellence. Really, it's a matter of programming our minds with the kind of information that will set us free. Free to be all God meant us to be. Free to soar! It will take awhile, and it may be painful-but what a metamorphosis!

Sid the Caterpillar

Sid was an ugly caterpillar with orange eyes. He spent his life groveling and squirming in the dirt on God's earth. One day Sid got a terrible idea. He crawled up the stem of a bush, made his way to a branch, and secreted a translucent fluid onto that branch. He made a kind of button out of the fluid, turned himself around, and attacked his posterior anatomy to that button. Then he shaped himself into a "J," curled up, and proceeded to build a house around himself. There was a lot of activity for a while, but before long Sid was entirely covered up and you couldn't see him anymore.

Everything became very, very still. You might have concluded that nothing at all was happening. But, as a matter of fact, plenty was happening. Metamorphosis was taking place.

One day Sid began to raise the window shades of his house. He let you look in and see a variety of colors. On another day an eruption took place. Sid's house shook violently. That little cocoon jerked and shook until a large, beautiful wing protruded from one of the windows. Sid stretched it out in all its glory. He continued his work until another gorgeous wing emerged from a window on the other side of the house.

At this stage of Sid's life you might have wanted to

help. But you didn't, for if you tried to pull the rest of Sid's house off you would maim him for the rest of his life. So you let Sid convulse and wriggle his way to freedom without any outside intervention.

Eventually Sid got his house off his back, ventured out onto the branch, stretched, and spread his beautiful wings. He was nothing like the old worm he used to be. And do you know what? Sid did not crawl back down the bush and start groveling and squirming in the dirt again. No indeed! Instead, he took off with a new kind of power-flight power. Now, instead of swallowing dust, Sid flies from flower to flower, enjoying the sweet nectar in God's wonderful creation.

Perhaps you read those words with a sigh: "Well, that may be the way it is for a caterpillar named Sid, but somehow I just don't qualify; flight power sounds stimulating, but I'm made for mediocrity, swallowing dust not sniffing flowers." Hogwash! With that kind of attitude, you've managed to think your way out of the very things you long to enjoy. You have become what you've been thinking. No wonder your metamorphosis is on hold![3]

The Mind: Target of the Enemy

Let me get to the heart of the issue. Since the mind holds the secrets of soaring, the enemy of our souls has made the human mind the bull's eye of his target. His most insidious and strategic moves are made upon the mind. By affecting the way we think, he is able to keep our lives on a defeated level. There are a couple of extremely significant sections in the New Testament that address Satan's scheming nature. Let us look at Ephesians 6:10-11.

"Finally, be strong in the Lord, and in the strength of His might. Put on the full armor of God, that you may be able to stand firm against the schemes of the devil."

Notice those four final words: **"Schemes of the devil."** The Greek term translated **"schemes"** is METHODIA, from which we get our English word method. The Amplified Bible captures the correct idea by rendering it **"strategies of the devil."** He has a well-thought-through strategy, time-honored and effective-a plan that works like a charm. To understand it we need to remember that the battle is not in the visible realm. "For our struggle is not against flesh and blood..." (Eph. 6:12). The struggle (that's a good word for it, isn't it?) is not a flesh-and-blood struggle. It's not tangible; its mental-it is simply not in the realm of something we can see, touch, or hear.

Paul says, "But whom you forgive anything, I forgive also; for indeed what I have forgiven, if I have forgiven anything, I did it for your sakes in the presence of Christ, in order that no advantage be taken of us by Satan; for we are not ignorant of his schemes (2 Cor. 2:10-11). Obviously, the larger subject here is forgiveness. Those people in ancient Corinth were being chided because they had half forgiven a fellow in their church. By failing to forgive fully, they provided Satan with an "advantage," an opportunity to infiltrate and demoralize them. Note that the writer Paul adds a most insightful comment: "...we are not ignorant of his "schemes" was the root word for "method." But here the Greek term comes from a root word meaning the "mind." Satan plays mind games with us, and unless we're clued in, he will win! Maybe Paul as not ignorant of the devil's mind-oriented strategy, but most people I meet are.

> **And even if our gospel is veiled, it is veiled to those who are Perishing, in whose case the god of this world has blinded the Minds of the unbelieving, that they might not see the light of The gospel of the glory of Christ, who is the image of God (2 Cor. 4:3-4).**

Once again we find the enemy (called here "the god of this world") working in his favorite territory, the mind. Those who live in unbelief do so because he has "blinded the minds of the unbelieving." Many-in fact, most-live their lives in spiritual blindness. It's as if a thick, dark veil were draped across their thinking to keep them from seeing the light. Only the power of Christ can penetrate that veil and bring light and hope and happiness. Paul describes this so vividly a couple of verses later:

> **For God, who said, "Light shall shine out of darkness," is the one who has shone in our hearts to give the light of the knowledge of the glory of God in the face of Christ (2 Cor. 4:6).**

But don't think for a moment that the enemy relinquishes his long held territory without a fight, a fight that endures throughout life! Everything being described in 2 Corinthians 10:3-5 occurs in the mind.

Clearly, the scenes of battle are woven through these lines. You can almost smell smoke and hear the reports of massive weapons, except for one problem-it isn't a "war according to the flesh." It's a mind-oriented struggle, a "warfare...not of the flesh." It all takes place in the invisible, intangible realm of the mind.

For though we walk in the flesh, we do not war according to the flesh, for the weapons of our warfare are not of the flesh, but divinely powerful for the destruction of the fortresses. We are destroying speculations and every lofty thing raised up against the knowledge of God, and are taking every thought captive to the obedience of Christ (2 Cor. 10:3-5).

In ancient days cities were built within thick, massive walls. The wall provided a formidable barrier that protected the city, holding the enemy at bay. Before any alien force could expect to conquer a city, it first had to overcome that protective shield. Towers were even erected in strategic places within the wall. In times of battle, seasoned men with an understanding of military warfare would position themselves in those stations that towered above the surrounding wall...In order for the enemy to take the city, three objectives had to be accomplished. First, the wall had to be scaled or penetrated. Second, the towers had to be invaded. Third, the men of military strategy had to be captured. In 2 Corinthians 10, we have this very principle illustrated-not in a city, but in the mind.

Satan doesn't want to give up the territory of the mind. He is a defeated foe who knows his future. But he fights to the last degree to maintain the hold he has had on us. His "stronghold" reveals itself in our humanistic nature-in the habits we established back then, and the whole lifestyle we lived under enemy command. This is one of the reasons that those who become Christians later in life have such tremendous battles in the realm of the mind... In order for the truth of God to win, ...our minds have to be penetrated. How does that happen? The Lord brings a divinely powerful weapon, the Holy Spirit, with His magnificent armory of truths from scripture. His remarkable filling, and dynamic empowering. Once the Lord breaks through the wall-like fortress and speculations, He encounters those "lofty things" the mental blocks we've erected. You and I are prompted to go back to carnal habits when under pressure, when under attack, when undergoing a test, when doing without, when persecuted, when maligned, criticized, or done wrong. Our tendency is to rely on those traditional "lofty things"-those established thoughts that were passed on to us by our parents, our friends, and our colleagues. Such mental blocks are carnal to the core. ...God is interested in our breaking free from such mental blocks. He realizes each "lofty thing" has dug in its heels and must be dislodged. As we often say, "Old habits are hard to break." For too many years, we have convinced ourselves that we lack this or we cannot do that...we should not risk...we are sure to fail...we ought to accept the status quo as our standard. But these programmed "lofty things" must be conquered!

And what is God's ultimate goal? Just as we read in 2 Corinthians 10:5-to take "every thought captive." When he invaded those lofty areas, His plan is to transform the old thought patterns that defeat us into new thoughts that encourage us. He has to repattern our whole way of thinking. And He is engaged in doing that continually because old habits are so hard to break...Finally, you have some insight on your battle with lust, or envy, or pride, or jealousy, or extreme perfection, or a negative, critical spirit...God's offer is nothing short of phenomenal! Remember it? It is taking every thought captive to the obedience of Christ." Or, as one paraphrase reads:

It is true that we live in the world, but we do not fight from worldly motives. The weapons we use in our fight are not the world's weapons but God's powerful weapons, which we use to destroy strongholds. We destroy false arguments; we pull down every proud obstacle that is raised against the knowledge of God; we take every thought captive and make it obey Christ (2 Cor. 10:3-5 TEV).[4]

Renewing Your Mind

In the book, "The Mind of Christ" it says, "The mind has always been important to God than our outward actions. In the Old Testament, the emphasis was on the heart. At times, the Bible uses the word heart where we would use the word mind as in injunction, "Apply your heart to discipline" (Proverbs 23:12). In the New Testament, Jesus used the word heart in the same sense: "And Jesus knowing their thoughts said, "Why are you thinking evil in your hearts?" (Matt. 9:4). Most of us, most of the time, are satisfied if we satisfy the expectations of society and the requirements of God by our outer, visible actions. God looks on the inner; He said, as early as Samuel's day, that "man looks at the outward appearance, but the Lord looks at the heart" (I Sam. 16:7)......The Old Testament places little emphasis on our becoming like God while the New Testament reiterates numerous injunctions to imitate God or to be like Christ. In earliest pages, the Bible tells that God created us in His image (Gen. 1:26-27; 5:1). Yet after Adam's fall, the Old Testament has very little reference to our likeness to God and no admonitions to become like Him. The Old Testament emphasis is on the difference between God and Man, "For my thoughts are not your thoughts, Neither are your ways My ways, : declares the Lord, "for as the heavens are higher than the earth, So are My ways higher than your ways. And My thoughts than your thoughts" (Isa. 55:8-9). Apart from Christ, our ways today are not His ways. The Odd Testament idea was that God molds us and shapes us from the outside: "We are the clay, and Thou our potter; And all of us are the work of Thy hand" (Isa. 64:8). The New Testament makes a racial shift in its emphasis. Here it is, "Christ in us the Hope of Glory.".......Our minds are clustered with information. Our thought life has been send by the world a constant barrage of messages to us-politics, world, business, sex, sports, products and others. God also is sending us messages, messages about His expressed will in the Bible for us, promptings about words to say or not to say, anger to control, or patience to extend.... Many people choose to follow vacantly the world track of messages coming in, regardless of their source. On the other hand, we can reject some of them or even cut off their source.... The New Testament gives three specific commands-that concern the mind. These scriptural mandates give us the clues necessary to discern how to think in the same way that Christ thought. The three commands can be classified as the beginning, middle, and ending stages of a process that culminates in spiritual maturity.

The Will Principle

The first principle, or the beginning of the process, is found in Colossians 3:2: "Set your mind on the things above, not on the things that are on the earth." Paul is stating a principle-The Will Principle. We must **"set"** our mind. ....The will is part of our mind in which we have control. "We are taking every thought captive to the obedience of Christ" (2 Cor. 10:5). The will enables us to obey in spite of feeling. Often we cannot control our emotions, but we always have control over the will. Our identification with Christ must began here or not at all....The verb **"set"** comes first because Christ identified His will with the Father...When we set our will and become like Christ, God will purify our resolve.

The River Principle

The second New Testament verb, or command, that is used with the word **"mind"** is in Romans 12:2: "Be transformed by the renewing of your mind." The Christian is actually lives in a constant state of renewal! After we give our will to God, we must continue this process.

In the command to be transformed by the renewing of our mind, we have another principle-the River Principle. Our growth is like the flow of a river, Jesus said, "He who believes in Me, as the Scripture said, "from his innermost being shall flow rivers of living water" (John 7:38). Our problem is that most of us do not work on the River Principle, we work on the Pond Principle, Ponds stagnate, but rivers flow. Ponds becomes puddles but rivers becomes oceans. We are to grow in the word. Allowing the Holy Spirit to renew our thinking through the word of God and producing in us newness.

The Readiness Principle

Our third verb-command associated with the mind takes us to the climax of the process: "Gird up your minds for action" (I Peter 1:13). In the first century people wore long flowing robes. To run or move quickly, a person had to turn the robe into a kind of pantaloon by "girding up" the robe. This illustrates the Readiness principle. Our minds are to remain prepared for action." [5]

Having the mind of Christ is having the eagle mentality!

Breakthrough-Questions and Answers for Growth

1. What one area do you need to develop your eagle mentality?

_____

_____

_____

_____

_____

_____

2. What area can you be more tenacious for Christ?

_____

_____

_____

_____

_____

_____

3. Are all the people that you are hanging with are healthy for you?

_____

_____

_____

_____

_____

_____

_____

_____

4. In what ways can you be more nurturing in your relationships?

_____

_____

_____

_____

_____

_____

_____

_____

5. Are you asking God for more vision and insight into your present situation (explain)?

_____

_____

_____

_____

_____

_____

_____

_____

6. What present challenge do you need courage?

_____

_____

_____

_____

_____

_____

_____

Chapter 2 –
Discovery and Growth

That's how life is! God stirs up your nest, but in stirring up your nest, you discover who God is and who you are! In Isaiah 40:28 we discover seven things (attributes) about God:

> Isaiah 40:28, "Have you not known? Have you not heard? The everlasting God, the Lord, the Creator of the ends of the earth, neither faints nor is weary. His understanding is unsearchable."

Discover Who God Is

It is important to know the nature of the one you are dealing with. Knowing the nature of God as He reveals Himself in the word of God will indeed bless you. Bunnies hop because it is their nature. Cows moo because it is their nature. Lions roar because it is their nature. Cats catch birds because it is their nature. Dogs chase cats because it is their nature. That's just what they do. You don't have to prod them to do it, you don't have to encourage them to do it, you don't have to teach them to do it. It's part of what they are.

When we talk about the nature of God, we are speaking of the characteristics intrinsic to His being. What does He do naturally?

To some people God appears a tyrant, so they are waiting for their next whipping. To others, He's a joke. To still others, God seems like a nice grandfather with a long, white beard, kind of gentle to be around but with little influence. Or He's just a bigger, better version of man. But if we are going to have an intimate walk with God, we must understand what makes Him tick-His true nature. As you consider the character of God, His nature it will help you grasp the greatness of God.[6]

Everlasting God

Our great God is eternal. Moses declared: **Lord, Thou hast been our dwelling place in all generations. Before the mountains were born, or Thou didst give birth to the earth and the world, even from everlasting to everlasting, Thou art God (Psalms 90:1-2)**

God Has No Beginning
"From everlasting to everlasting"- that is a long time! When did God begin? From everlasting-but if you exist from everlasting you have no starting point. To put it another way, there has never been a time when God was not. Now don't try to figure that one out or it will drive you stark raving mad.

God existed from everlasting. There never was a time when God was not, and there will never be a time when

God will not be. It is very important to realize that God is forever. This truth has a fundamental implication for us. With God, there is no such thing as the succession of events. History is a meaningless concept to Him. We are creatures of history because we are linear creatures. By that I mean we go from point A to point B to point C, from one to ten. We go from event to that event to the next event, one after the other. We are creatures of the past, the present, and the future. We are linear, successive creatures, but that is irrelevant to God. He knows about history because He's the God of history, but history doesn't control Him. Remember that He told Moses, "I Am Who I Am."

All of us have attended a parade, which we see as a succession of events. We stand on the curb and watch a float pass by, then a band, followed by a drill team, one after the other. At best, you can look down the street and see two or three successive events at a time. But you can't see around all the corners or see the full length of the parade because it is linear. It moves down the street from point A to point B.

However, if you were to go aloft in the Goodyear blimp, it would be a new deal. From overhead you can see the whole parade in one grand sweep. The succession of events becomes irrelevant from the blimp because you are so high up looking so far down that it's all one event. You and I live from today to tomorrow to next month to next year. But God sits in the Goodyear blimp. He sees the whole thing as one because he's from everlasting to everlasting.

God Is Independent

The eternality of God also means, as we've seen already, that God is independent. Everything created needs something outside of itself to exist. But God depends on nothing outside Himself to exist. He is self-generating. Jesus taught in John 5:26, "the Father hath life in himself." Now I've got good news and bad news. The bad news is God does not need us. He did not create us out of any need or lack in His Person. Before there was earth or anything else, God was. When earth was created, God had already existed millions of years. In fact, even that is an understatement, since one can go back into eternity forever and never find a time when God did not exist. How did He make it that long without us? Because God needs nothing outside of Himself to be Himself or to be complete. He is totally self-generating. He is totally fulfilled within Himself.

The good news is that God created us so we could get in on what He is enjoying: Himself. He created us so that we can enjoy Him, benefit from Him, and participate in His world, not to make up for something that was lacking. God does not need man, and so man can't threaten Him.[7]

The Lord

This word Lord is the Hebrew word "Jehovah" which means the existing One." Also it is the proper name of the one true God. "God is Himself the Almighty God. He must needs be so, for He is everlasting God, even Jehovah. He was from eternity, He will be to eternity; and therefore with him there is no deficiency, no decay. He has His being of Himself, and therefore all His perfections must be boundless. He is without beginning of days or end of life, and therefore with Him there is no change."[8]

The Creator

The word creator is the Hebrew word "bara'" which means to create, shape and form (always with God as subject) of heaven and earth; of individual man; of new conditions and circumstances and of transformations. "God is the creator of the ends of the earth, that is, of the whole earth and all that is in it from end to end. He is therefore the rightful owner and ruler of all, and must be concluded to have an absolute power over all and an all-sufficiency to help His people in their greatest straits."[9]

God Never Faints or Gets Weary

God has power to bring about the salvation and the power is never exhausted: He faints not, nor is He weary; He upholds the whole creation, and governs all the creatures, and he is neither tired nor toiled; and therefore. No doubt, He has the power to relieve His people when we are brought low. [10]

God is all powerful! This attribute is called the "omnipotence of God." His omnipotence involves more than just using raw power. God's omnipotence includes the exercise of His choice to use His unlimited power to reflect His divine glory and accomplish His sovereign will.... God is unlimited in what He can do. He is unlimited in how He gets it done. God's power is so limitless that He can create ex nihilo, meaning "out of nothing." God's unlimited power is effortless. He doesn't strain, grunt, or groan. He doesn't get sweaty because something is too hard to lift or too difficult to make.

> **Ah Lord God! Behold, Thou hast made the heavens and the earth by Thy great power and by Thine outstretched arm! Nothing is too difficult for Thee. (Jeremiah 32:17)**

God's Understanding is Unsearchable

When we talk about God's understanding that is called the "omniscience of God." That word is made up of two words; omni, which means: "all" and science, which has to do with "knowledge." So when we talk about the omniscience of God, we are referencing to His "all-knowingness," what God knows. This refers to His perfect knowledge of all things both actual and potential. There is absolutely nothing that God doesn't know, that no informational system or set of data exists anywhere outside of God's knowledge-nothing. He depends on no one outside Himself for any knowledge about anything. That's so unlike us.

We are all dependent on someone else's knowledge. In fact, we sometimes stake our lives on the fact that someone knows something. Every time you fill a prescription at the pharmacy, you bank on the fact that the person behind that counter is not a fool. You trust your life to the assumption that your pharmacist went to school and that he doesn't confuse medicines. Very few of us ever check on it. We don't open up the pills to make sure they contain the right medicinal ingredients. We wouldn't know them if we saw them anyway. We know only that the doctor wrote the prescription, the pharmacist filled it, and we are going to shallow it. We depend on the knowledge of others.

In Isaiah 40:13-14, the prophet gives us this very valuable piece of information about God's perfect knowledge:

Who has directed the Spirit of the Lord, or as His counselor has informed Him? With whom did He consult and who gave Him understanding? And who taught Him in the path of justice and taught Him knowledge, and informed Him of the way of understanding?

To put it in our terms, where did the Lord go to school? Isaiah raises the question to illustrate a fundamental principle, that God does not gain knowledge by learning. He does not need to study, read, and analyze. He knows what he knows simply because He knows it.. ...Because God is eternal, whatever He knows, He knows immediately and simultaneously. All knowledge past, present and future resides in Him in the eternal now. All that is known, has been known, will be known, could be known, or has been forgotten, God knows intuitively and eternally...All the information in all the libraries of the world; all the data on all the computer chips in the world, including the chips that have not yet been made; all of this data, God knows perfectly and completely right now. Because He is infinite, "His understanding is infinite" (Psalms 147:5).... Nothing can be hidden from God. He knows your feelings, your desires, your excuse, and your personality.

He knows everything and anything, and He knows it comprehensively. Hebrews 4:13: "there is no creature hidden from His sight, but all things are open and laid bare to the eyes of Him with whom we have to do." God's knowledge includes a moral element. Proverbs 15:3 says that "the eyes of the Lord are in every place, watching the evil and the good." Nothing escape His all encompassing knowledge-not the biggest or the minute detail. He even knows the very hairs on our heads (Matthew 10:30) and that even one sparrow will fall to the ground apart from God's knowledge (Matthew 10:29)."

Are not two sparrows sold for a penny? Yet not one of them will fall to the ground apart from the will of your Father. And even the very hairs of your head are all numbered. So don't be afraid; you are worth more than many sparrows (Matthew 10:29-31). NIV

Discover Who You Are

No matter what circumstances you are in, remember who God is! Remember who you are in Christ! Discovery is awesome! I'm still discovering things about God in my relationship with Him and I am still discovering things about myself **in Christ!** The eagle experiences season of discovery and growth. This season of your life is a season of discovery. You will discover like the eagle that you can fly... that God has given you within the ability to soar! **Christian Counseling (International Institute of Faith Based Counseling) Manuel** states on pages 82-88, "Throughout the ages there have been primarily four questions that man has asked. They are:

1. **Who am I?**
2. **Where is my place in life?**

3. **What do I do with my life?**
4. **Is there any meaning or eternal value to life?**

As people journey through life, they look for the answers to these questions, usually without even consciously forming the questions in their minds. They may wonder what to do with their life and may feel as though their life has no meaning. Without answers, they look to something or someone to which they may attach themselves to in hopes of finding fulfillment and satisfaction.

Their quest to **"find"** themselves or their attempt to fit into a family system or culture often leads them to accept less than God's best for them. Looking to the "world system" for fulfillment, they are often lured into accepting the counterfeit idols of this world such as sex, money, fame, relationships, power, or success. Never finding true satisfaction to these substitutes, they continue to search for what their human spirit truly longs for-God and His plan to their lives.

These same four questions can be more clearly defined as:

1. What is my **identity?**
2. What is my **position?**
3. What is my **purpose?**
4. What is the **significance?**

These questions are spiritual in nature and can only to understood in relationship to our original glory-that which we were before the Fall of man. When Adam was created, he was created with great glory and honor. He was God's friend and he fellowshipped with God in the garden (**identity**). God gave Adam dominion and authority over the garden, the animals and all the works of His hand (**position**), and then commanded Adam to be fruitful and multiply (**purpose**). Adam found great meaning and value in pleasing God (**significance**).

As Adam walked into his destiny in the fullness of his identity, position, purpose and significance, Adam experienced true life and fulfillment and thus brought great glory to God, his Creator. When sin entered into the picture, Adam lost his true identity and destiny; however, there is no true identity, position, purpose, significance outside God. No identity, position, purpose, and significance outside of God only produces:

- **Low self - esteem**
- **Confusion**
- **No hope**
- **Co-dependency**
- **No fulfillment**
- **No meaning to life**
- **No power**

There are many Christians struggling to know their identity and to walk in the fullness of their identity, position, purpose and significance in Christ. Many Christians have a grasp of their identity and position in Christ but do not have a grasp of their purpose or significance, simply because they have never yielded to transformation (Romans 12:2). When an individual's life is not surrendered to God, their needs remain unsettled. Identity and significance have more to do with our relationship with Christ, while position and purpose have more to do with being productive for Christ. All life is about having relationship and being productive.

What is my Identity?
- My identity is defined in Christ and my relationship to Him.
- I am a child of God
- I have God as my father
- I am forgiven of all my sins.
- I have eternal security in the family of God

What is my position?
- My position is defined with Christ
- I am seated at the right hand of the father in Christ
- Christ has given me power and dominion
- I am a citizen of heaven accepted in the beloved
- I have direct access to God
- I have power over my carnal nature and over the forces of evil in this earth
- I am more than a conqueror through Christ

What is my purpose?
- My purpose is defined as His specific will for my life
- I am God's co-worker and have been created for good works
- I am chosen and appointed to bear fruit
- I am a minister of reconciliation and an ambassador for Christ
- Christ has given me a job to do and the power to accomplish it

What is the significance?

- I am what I do, have eternal significance with eternal rewards for appreciation
- God is please with those who do good and He will not forget your labor of love
- My toil is not in vain and others will receive eternal life because I share the good news with them
- My efforts produce an eternal weight of glory
- My life has meaning and value to God and that makes me want to please Him
- My life really matters and it matters to God and that gives me passion to serve Him

Your Identity is "In Christ"

The New Testament, mainly in the epistles written to the church, phrases and prepositions like IN CHRIST, IN HIM, WITH CHRIST, THROUGH CHRIST, IN WHOM, BY CHRIST, BY HIM, OF HIM, THROUGH HIM, WITH HIM, IN HIS NAME, etc. expresses to us what God has revealed exactly who we are and what we have already (past tense) become because of the redemptive work of Jesus Christ. The reason why the **"IN CHRIST"** scriptures are so important is because all your victories, all your blessings, freedom, deliverance from Satan are already yours **"IN CHRIST."** There are 111 **"IN CHRIST"** phrases in the New Testament.

- Being justified freely by his grace through the redemption that is **in Christ Jesus**. (Romans 3:24)

- Likewise reckon ye also yourselves to be dead indeed unto sin, but alive unto God **through Jesus Christ** our Lord. (Romans 6:11)

- For the law of the Spirit of life **in Christ Jesus** hath made me free from the law of sin and death. (Romans 8:2)

- There is therefore now no condemnation to them which are **in Christ Jesus**, who walk not after the flesh, but after the Spirit. (Romans 8:1)

- Nor height nor depth, nor any other creature, shall be able to separate us from the love of God, which is **in Christ Jesus** our Lord. (Romans 8:39)

- So we, being many, are one body **in Christ**, and every one members one of another (Romans 12:5)

- I thank my God at all times for you because of the grace (the favor and spiritual blessing) of God which was bestowed on you **in Christ Jesus** (I Corinthians 1:4) Amplified Bible

- Now he which established us with you **in Christ**, and hath anointed us, is God; (2 Corinthians 1:21)

- Now thanks be unto God, which always causes us to triumph **in Christ**, and maketh manifest

the savour of his knowledge by us in every place
(2 Corinthians 2:14)

- Therefore if any man be **in Christ**, he is a new creature: old things have passed away; behold all things are become new. (2 Corinthians 5:17)

- For ye are all children of God by faith **in Christ Jesus**. (Galatians 6:26)

- Blessed be the God and Father of our Lord Jesus Christ, who hath blessed us with all spiritual blessings in heavenly places **in Christ**. (Ephesians 1:3)

- And hath raised us up together, and made us sit together in heavenly places **in Christ Jesus** (Ephesians 2:6)

- For we are his workmanship, created **in Christ Jesus** unto good works, which God hath before ordained that we should walk in them. (Ephesians 2:10)

- Let this mind be in you, which was also **in Christ Jesus**. (Philippians 2:5)

- And God's peace (shall be yours, that tranquil state of a soul assured of its salvation **through Christ**, and so fearing nothing from God and being content with its earthly lot of whatever sort that is, that peace) which transcends all understanding shall garrison and mount guard over your hearts and minds **in Christ Jesus**. (Philippians 4:7) Amplified Bible

- And my God shall supply all your need according to his riches in glory **in Christ Jesus**. (Philippians 4:13)

- And you are complete **in Him**, which is the head of all principality and power. (Colossians 2:10)

- For the Lord himself shall descend from heaven with a shout, with the voice of the archangel, and with the trump of God: and the dead **in Christ** shall rise first: (1 Thessalonians 4:16)

- In everything give thanks: for this is the will of God **in Christ Jesus** concerning you. (1 Thessalonians 5:18)

- Who hath saved us, and called us with an holy calling, not according to our works, but according to his own purpose and grace, which was given us **in Christ Jesus** before the world began (2 Timothy 1:9)

- And after you have suffered a little while, the God of all grace (who imparts all blessing and favor), who has called you to His (own) eternal glory **in Christ Jesus**, will Himself complete and make you what you ought to be, establish and ground you securely, and strengthen, and settle you. (1 Peter 5:10) Amplified Bible

- If anyone says, I love God, and hates (detests, abominates) his brother **(in Christ)**, he is a liar; for he who does not love his brother, whom he has seen, cannot love God, whom he has not seen. (1 John 4:20) Amplified Bible

CeCe Winans says in her song "Up Where I Belong"
Lord lift me up where we belong!

Where the eagles fly on the mountain high
Lord lift us up where we belong
Up from the worlds we know
Where the clear winds blow

Breakthrough-Questions
and Answers for Growth

1. What new thing are you discovering in your relationship with God in the last twelve months?

   _____

   _____

   _____

   _____

   _____

   _____

   _____

2. What new thing have you discovered about yourself
   through your last crisis?

   _____

   _____

   _____

   _____

   _____

   _____

   _____

3. What do you know now about yourself because of your last triumph?

_____

_____

_____

_____

_____

_____

_____

_____

_____

_____

_____

_____

Chapter 3 – Broken Wings

Eagles represent independence, responsibility, strength, freedom, keenness of vision, rarity, and a dozen other admirable traits that we wish to emulate. But, though strong of heart and awesome on wing, eagles are not super birds incapable of being captured or immune to accident or disease. Like all other creatures, they have weaknesses. They can make mistakes, misjudge distances, and miscalculate dives. Falling victim to such perils can leave them with broken bones, earthbound and defenseless. We seldom think of eagles in such vulnerable conditions. Can you remember the last time you saw a photograph or drawing of a helpless eagle? The eagle is always portrayed in graceful flight or diving for the kill, never in the claws or mouth of its captor. But to the contrary eagles have weaknesses .Just like you and I they become grounded and experiences broken wings.[12]

In Isaiah 40:28-29, we are told that there is the reality of getting faint and having no strength at times. This season is for real! God says that you and I get **weak and** we have no **strength.** The word of God continues to teach us that,

"Even the youth will faint and get weary and the young men will utterly fall!" Sometimes you are just exhausted by life's battles.

> **Isaiah 40:29-30, "He gives power to the weak and to those who have no might He increases strength. Even the youths shall faint and be weary, and the young men shall utterly fall."**

Too Tired to Fly

You are weak! You are tired! You are faint! You are depleted! Have you ever felt that you have no more spiritual resources! Have you ever felt you can't go on or even one more step? Sometimes you feel that you just don't have no more strength to continue to work in the kingdom! Sometimes you are just weak, worn and exhausted! You are experiencing spiritual burnout!

The Dynamic Duo (Power and Strength)

Even though you are an eagle, you get tired, broken and weary. But also in verses 29-30, God gives two dynamic spiritual forces. In verse 29, He gives **power** to the weak (faint)! That word **power** is translated into seven (7) different words, (strength, might, force, ability, able, substance and wealth). God gives power to the faint!

> **Exodus 15:6, "Thy right hand, O Lord is become glorious in power."**

Numbers 14:17, "Now, let the power of the Lord be great."

God will give you power when you get weak and faint! It is a spiritual Power! That word "power" in the Hebrew is the word "koach" which means Secondly, in verse 29... He will increase strength! That word "Strength" in the Hebrew is the word "otsmah" which means to This strength will help you to walk through whatever. One writer says, "There must be a switch from your **human battery** to the **infinite power** of God." When "grief" comes in your life, God will switch you from your human battery to His infinite power!

Actually, what God does, "He exchanges your strength and He gives you His strength." It is not your strength anymore but its' God's strength! Jesus said in 2 Corinthian 12:9, "My strength is made perfect in weakness." That's why you do not harm yourself! The danger is depending on other resources to give you strength! Destructive behavior! Substances to give you a high!

Identifying Strongholds

There are areas of bondage that are very damaging: certain habits, loyalties, relationships, prejudices, ambitions, duties, debt, possessions, fears, weaknesses, and hurts. Anyone can be free in the areas I have described. God's intention is that we are free from this world's mind-set. If you would make a list of these areas and allow for concentration and much prayer. You will discover the encouragement of seeing God work in these areas. Jesus Christ was the freest human being who ever walked on earth. As His ministry moved into various phases. He had to make decisions-ministry decisions, decisions about what to say and when to say it, where to go and when to go, always watching the timing of His Father. Christ's freedom within us facilities the mental quality of attention-attention to God, to His word, to prayer, and to His voice. God's goal is our freedom.

Little by little, God transforms our mind-set to a God mindset. In all these transformations, we are being set free-freed from false conceptions. **Not only are you being set free from but you are being set free to act-freed to let God have first place, freed to minister to His body, freed to move into new and deeper lessons on Christlikeness. Previously, outside forces have dictated the structure of your thought life. But now the Holy Spirit is desiring to direct your thoughts from within. Your thoughts are being repatterned by the word! Remember that God works in process, and sometimes that is very slow. Making lists and remaking lists and giving them to God facilities the process of "perfecting holiness" (2 Cor. 7:1). In the process, God is transforming your mind into the mind of Christ.**

The Mind of Christ

Have you ever evaluated the condition of your mind? Below is an inventory of two opposing sets of mental states. This evaluation is only for your information. Do it in absolute privacy, with no one but the lord and you knowing your performance that this stage. You will not score this exercise. Its sole purpose is to help you know what your mind is like present. [13]

Evaluation of Your Current Spiritual Mental State

(The Mind of Christ by T.W. Hunt)

Jealousy or envy_____Rejoicing in the success of your brother or sister in Christ

Breakthrough-Questions and Answers for Growth

1. Are you feeling spiritually weak or spiritually strong (explain)?

_____

_____

_____

_____

_____

_____

_____

2. Do you feel that you are growing spiritually as you should be?

_____

_____

_____

_____

_____

_____

_____

3. What are you discerning that God is desiring to build in you right now?

_____

_____

_____

_____

_____

_____

_____

_____

4. What broken area in your life that needs fixing and healing?

_____

_____

_____

_____

_____

_____

_____

_____

Chapter 4 –
The Molting Season

God calls us to wait upon Him! How does this work? Isaiah 40:31 says, "They that wait upon the Lord!" That word wait is the word expectancy. There is an expectancy that will cause peace of mind, trust and confidence in God! You see, the eagle, every year grows new feathers! Every year! But the eagle have to go through a painful life changing process called "molting" if he is to live . This process is so painful and traumatic that all eagles do not (survive) this process of molting.

The eagle's life takes a tremendous toil on him after about thirty years and he becomes overwhelmed and weary. His feathers get old and hard! His feet (claws) don't work with effectiveness! His beak bends! His eyes get grow dim! His body begins to breakdown! He can't defend himself anymore! He gets weak and can't eat or hunt for food! He can't fly! The eagle becomes sick and worn down! The eagle can't shed tears. His tear ducts dry out.

Transformation Process

But God has a transformation process called "Molting". In this process, the eagle pulls off his feathers, files down his beak and talons (claws). He is so weak that all he can do is cry out with a "molting sound". But the other old experienced eagles help him and they get meat and worms and swoop down and drop the molting bird some fresh food! They protect Him and keep the buzzards away and guard the "molting eagle".

This molting process takes about 150 days for the eagle to grow new feathers and for his beak to grow healthy! It takes about 150 days for his feet (claws) to heal. It takes about 150 days for the eagle to renew his strength. You see, sometimes, people will ask you "what's wrong? " They say, "You look bad!" They say, "Something is wrong!" You should answer, "I'm going through my molting season! I'm growing new feathers! I'm growing new teeth! I'm losing so that I might grow!"

Jeremiah

I noticed my grandson Jeremiah when he was five years old that he lost his two front teeth. He had a new look as he gave his sunshine smile. My wife Trish took his picture with his missing front teeth on her Samsung Gallery phone and forwarded his picture to her family and friends. We all for a while got a good laugh at his new look. Although Jeremiah lost his front teeth but in a few months there were brand new ones that grew back! This is a natural process in child development (molting season). Surely you will experience loss but God is going to renew you!

Experiencing Loss

Loss is evitable in the molting process. For the eagle to live it must experience loss. Life is about living with passion and purpose, but when that living is disrupted by the loss of someone or something important we are bound to feel an emotional letdown and some degree of distress. Like it or not, we all experience loss in our lives. Sometimes life is just flat out hard and our pain becomes almost unbearable.

Detox Negative Thoughts and Behaviors

There are areas of damaging emotions, thoughts and behaviors that are destructive in our lives producing bondages. Hurts, grudges, certain habits, unhealthy relationships, blind loyalties, prejudices, ambitions, duties, debt, possessions, fears, and weaknesses unchecked and left uncontrolled is the kryptonite for every Superman. . These damaging bondages can leave us trapped into the net of depression, despair, despondency and unforgiveness. These emotions and behaviors are dangerous and have the power to literally destroy our souls and spirits. Anyone can be set free in these areas. God's intention is that we be free from this world's mindset. In doing so God binds us to His mind-set and heals us everywhere that we hurt. By repatterning our thoughts and praying fervently one will experience the deeper working of the Holy Spirit in producing the fruit of the Spirit in our lives. If you begin the detox process, God has promised us to set us free from these destructive thought patterns and sin. Make the conscious decision to detox yourself from every negative influence in your life. This can be only done through the power of God's word in your life.

The eagle doing this molting process actually transforms from an old eagle to a new eagle. The many old destructive behaviors must be put away from you. While you are getting rid of the old, God is actually growing the new. The eagle retreats to a mountaintop and over a five month period goes through a metamorphosis. It knocks off its own beak by banging it against a rock, plucks out its talons and then feathers. Each stage produces a regrowth of the removed body parts, allowing the eagle to live for another 30-40 years. No wonder the Bible talks about God renewing our youth like the eagle.

Renewal Through Confession of Sin

Rick warren said in his Purpose Driven Connection Newsletter, "God uses all kinds of vessels-big vessels and little vessels, ornate vessels and plain vessels, very expensive ones. But there is one thing God will not use: a dirty vessel. So if you're going to be used by God, you have to do some cleanup. ...How do you do that? You do it through confession of sins. Augustine said, "The confession of bad works is the beginning of good works." We start by dealing with our past. The Bible says, 'If you confess your sins that He is faithful to forgive you of your sins and cleanse you from all righteousness. I John 1:9." I'll never forget the first time I made a "sin list." I felt like God was a million miles away, that he was at a distant. I couldn't feel his power or his grace. I felt like my prayers were bounding off the ceiling. So, one night I took out a yellow pad of paper and said, "God, show me every sin between me and you, and I will write it down specifically. I committed specifically. I'm going to deal with it right now and get it out of the way. I started writing. And writing. And writing. I thought I was going to write a book, like "The Purpose Driven Sinner" I ended up with about nine pages of sins. It was 2 a.m. when I finished. I confessed all those sins to God and wrote I John 1:9 over each. I've had to make a sin list many times since that night, because it is very easy to let things come between us and God. You need to make a sin list on a regular basis so that you can have a clean vessel to offer God for His use. If you only take the garbage out of your house once a month it's going to start stinking.

This molting process can be a time of confession and forsaken of sins. As you are giving God the old, He is creating something new and marvelous in your life.

Managing Your Emotions

Watchman Nee made two important statements about emotions in his book, Spiritual Man: 1). "Emotions may be denominated the most formidable enemy to the life of a Christian," and 2). "He therefore who lives by emotion lives without principle." What he was saying that we cannot be led by emotions. Yet our emotions will not go away doing this time of molting, we can learn to manage them. If we do not deal with them, these emotions will be our greatest enemy. More than anything, Satan uses our emotions against us from walking in the Spirit. We know the mind is the battlefield -the place where the battle is waged between the Spirit and the soul.

I can remember in the molting season of my life

battling through the deep emotions of rejection, depression, shame, anger, guilt and condemnation. These emotions began to rage within my soul like the mighty Niagara Falls. I struggled to see things from God perspective. But as God walked with me through this season He was in realty healing me and developing in my new strength. I was tempted to cater to these emotions and throw a daily pity party. But it was prayer, the word, worship, family and fellowship with other believers where I found that God's grace was sufficient for me. His grace sustained me and His grace will sustain you. In 2 Corinthians 12:9, "And He said to me, "My grace is sufficient for you, for My strength is made perfect in weakness." 'Therefore most gladly, I will rather boast in my infirmities, that the power of Christ may rest upon me.' The power of Christ kept me while His word nourished me. Like the eagle, God was growing new things in me. The eagle must go through this process because it is essential to his longevity. For four months a new eagle is emerging. This season of molting is a magnificent transformation for us as believers!

Renewal Through Forgiveness

Bruce Wilkinson in his book, "Experiencing Spiritual Breakthroughs" says, "Every pain or negative emotion becomes fertile ground for temptation and unless they are physically related, each one is rooted in an unresolved issue or event in our lives. As part of your journey of spiritual breakthroughs, I encourage you to begin asking God to reveal to you the cause of your inner distress. I promise you He will. Based on my experience and that of many others, I've found that an astounding 70 percent of our inner pain is rooted in unforgiveness."

Ephesians 4:31, "Let all bitterness, wrath, anger, clamor, evil speaking be put away from you, with all malice. And be kind to one another, tenderhearted, forgiving one another, even as God in Christ forgave you." (NKJV)

The Power of a Pure Heart

In "Let It Go" we read on pages 91-93, "Recorded in the Bible is a sermon Jesus delivered called the Beatitudes. During his delivery of these pearls of wisdom, he reveals one that I believe is essential of your healing journey to forgiveness, Jesus says, "Blessed are the pure in heart, for they shall see God" (Matthew 5:8), NIV). He indicated in this statement that the relationship between the status of our heart's condition and our ability to experience the divine. Jesus is basically telling us the secret to knowing God is spiritual housecleaning, realizing the importance of keeping your inner being free from clutter and debris. Understand that the heart spoken here isn't the one beating in your chest but is the core of your essence, your inner self, or your spirit. The term "pure" in this passage points to a term associated with catharsis, the removal of a blockage in order to restore freedom of movement. Now, if blockage of your physical heart is potentially lethal, so, too, is the clutter that can contaminate the valves and ventricles of your inner heart. The implication isn't that you can avoid experiencing such blockage, for Jesus warned us that "offenses will come." Instead Jesus's statement suggests that some people do not allow the offense to become plaque in the arteries of their creative inner being. Without life-threatening, soul-chocking constriction in their heart, these people experience the joy and freedom of an intimate relationship with their Creator. These people free themselves from long term emotional debilitation find themselves more blessed, more productive, and much more grounded than those who become blocked by incidents, tragedies, and injustices.

When you cling to past offenses, they cling to your heart and shorten your peaceful performance level by preventing you from exercising the ability to release the hurts and move on. No matter which soul-CPR method you employ, whether it be counseling, self-evaluation, or healthy confrontation, forgiveness is the gift you give yourself so that you can move forward. Rather than becoming stuck and forever tied to an adverse moment that you're constantly rehearsing, reliving, and resuffering, you can utilize forgiveness as a catheter to your heart. Jest as a medical catheter drains a physical part of toxic waste and flushes it out of the body, forgiveness siphons the toxic emotions away from the core of our being.

You see, in order to survive and forgive there must be a component of catharsis, a deep cleansing of the soul. Anytime there is emotion stagnancy, your inner health is jeopardized. Lingering issues left without resolution can become lethal to your well-being and block the blessings of creativity, opportunity, and openness to new experiences.

Often the process begins by confronting the truth within yourself, admitting that you are stuck in a state of reliving or rehearsing what you need to remove and release. You gain nothing by holding your offender as a hostage of your rage, demanding a ransom that they are often incapable of paying. Because in actuality, the only person you're holding hostage is yourself, and you are the only one who can ransom yourself through the power of forgiveness.

> **Mark 11:26-27, "And whenever you stand praying, if you have anything against anyone, forgive him, that your Father in heaven may also forgive you your trespasses. But if you do not forgive, neither will your Father in heaven forgive your trespasses."**

Preening

On that 150 day! Something else has grown, "oil sack" grows on the eagle's chest. That's call preening. Preening is the process by which birds groom and care for their feathers. When a bird is preening, she uses her beak to pick through feathers—removing any debris, arranging feathers that are out of place, and distributing a special oil that is secreted from a gland at the base of the tail. This oil helps a bird's feathers stay healthy and shiny. When the process is being manifested the oil sack on the eagle's chest is burst and the eagle oils his new feathers. (The oil protects and seals the feathers). While God is bringing you through your molting season, He is oiling you down with His precious Holy Spirit, who is strengthening you day by day.

The story is told by Jentezen Franklin of a couple in Southern California who lived in the foothills of the mountains. One day as they were hiking through a canyon, they noticed wild mushrooms growing everywhere. They decided to pick the mushrooms and take them home. They invited some friends over for a "mushroom party." No, they didn't smoke them; they cooked them. They sautéed the mushrooms, breaded them, and fried them. They made mushroom omelets, mushroom salad, and mushroom soup. They even concocted some mushroom desserts.

After dinner, as all of the guests were gathered at the table, having had a great time, the host went into the kitchen with leftovers. He had an old, lazy cat, so he decided to feed it with some scraps from the table. The cat gobbled up the mushrooms.

Sometime later, the host went back into the kitchen and found the cat lying on the floor, foaming at the mouth and panting for breath. He immediately phoned the veterinarian, who advised the man that he and his dinner guests had better get to the emergency room as soon as possible to have their stomachs pumped. The vet suspected that they had picked poisoned toadstools instead of mushrooms.

After going to the hospital and having their stomachs pumped, the people finally made it back home. They made their way into the kitchen, expecting to see their cat lying lifeless on the floor. Instead, the cat was in the corner of the kitchen with a brand-new litter of kittens!

Imagine that! Have you ever felt like that? What they thought were death pains were in reality birth pains!

The molting is about new life! With your new shine, new wings, new feathers, new feet, new beak and most important your new cleaned heart, you soar out into the atmosphere of possibilities and illuminate the darkness as an eagle.

Breakthrough-Questions and Answers for Growth

1. Describe the past and present molting season in your life?

   _____

   _____

   _____

   _____

   _____

   _____

   _____

2. What old things, habits and people is God moving out of your life?

   _____

   _____

   _____

   _____

   _____

   _____

   _____

3. What new things, habits and people is God placing in your life?

_____

_____

_____

_____

_____

_____

_____

_____

4. Are you having a difficult time in this transformation season of your life?

_____

_____

_____

_____

_____

_____

_____

_____

5. What one emotion are you dealing with right now?

_____

_____

_____

_____

_____

_____

_____

_____

6. Have you experienced the supernatural strength of God recently (explain)?

_____

_____

_____

_____

_____

_____

_____

_____

Chapter 5 –
Satisfying Your Mouth
With Good Things

The Bible has much to say about the mouth. Our mouths can either be a well of life or it can be a well of poison. God desires that our mouths be a well of life. In Psalms 103:5 it says, "God will satisfy your **mouth** with **good things** so that your youth is renewed like the eagle." Jesus is the ultimate example of how to use our mouths in the midst of circumstances. I Peter 2:21-22 says, "For to this you were called, because Christ also suffered for us leaving us, leaving us an example, that you should follow His steps. Who committed no sin, **nor was guile (deceit)** found in His mouth."

The word guile is defined as insidious cunning in attaining a goal; crafty or artful deception; duplicity. Jesus used His mouth always for the good. There is too much damage that we do with our mouth! How much guile, deceit, and duplicity is in your mouth. It's the stuff in your mouth that gets you in so much conflict and controversy.

"Solomon, author of the ancient Hebrew wisdom

literature, wrote, "The tongue has the power of life and death." Many people have never learned the tremendous power of verbally affirming each other. Solomon further noted, "An anxious heart weighs a man down, but a kind word cheers him up." [14]

> **Matthew 15:11, "Not what goes into the mouth defiles a man: but what comes out of the mouth, this defiles a man."**
>
> **Matthew 15:18-19, "But those things which proceed out of the mouth come out of the mouth come from the heart, and they defile a man. For out the heart proceed evil thoughts, murders, adulteries, fornications, thefts, false witness, blasphemies. These are the things which defile a man...."**
>
> **Proverbs 18:4, "The words of a man's mouth are deep waters, but the fountain of wisdom is a bubbling brook." (NIV)**
>
> **Proverbs 18:6, "A fool's lips bring him strife, and his mouth invites a beating." (NIV)**
>
> **Proverbs 18:7, "A fool's mouth is his undoing, and his lips are a snare to his soul." (NIV)**
>
> **Proverbs 18:8, "The words of a gossip are like choice morsels: they go down to a man's inmost parts." (NIV)**

Proverbs 18:20, "From the fruit of his mouth a man's stomach is filled; with the harvest from his lips he is satisfied." (NIV)

Proverbs 18:21, "The tongue has the power of life and death, and those who love it will eat its fruit." (NIV)

You are Responsible for Your Words

"Some of us have short fuses. There are persons in our lives that ignite our fuses. Some of us have long experience of holding our fusses out to be lit. Maybe you've said, "Sticks and stones my break my bones, but words will never hurt me!" But words can wound; they become the shrapnel ripping through the soul. In the heat of battle, words get by our lips, sometimes without ever having been near our brains. Sometimes with almost sadistic glee we have seen the words impact almost like bullets; we have seen others wince in pain." [15]

Jesus is the Ultimate Eagle

The gospel of John portrays Jesus as an Eagle. The gospel of Matthew portrays Jesus as a lion, the gospel of Mark as an ox, gospel of Luke as a man but the gospel of John Jesus is as an eagle, who is our savior whose wings that we fly. His one solidary life is without parallel.

Jesus is an eagle on the cross and dies as the lamb of God as our ultimate sacrifice for the remission of our sins. Nevertheless I see the eagle in Jesus coming out on the cross. One can see Psalms 103:5 being manifested as he suffered, bled and died.

The Eagle Beak Bends

The eagle after thirty years of existence, his beak bends. This makes it difficult for the eagle to grab his food and all other functions that has to do with him using his beak. During the season of molting this eagle with his bent beak finds a rock and begins to file down his beak so that he can use his mouth properly.

Jesus on the Cross

On the cross Jesus shows us how to use our mouth! It is said that the suffering, pain on the cross was so extreme that a person dying on the cross would curse and use insanities to the point of cursing their mothers and the day that they were born. Pain has a way of squeezing the flesh. Many times our mouths express the true nature of our hearts in the time of crisis.

Jesus is in a very vicarious situation of the cross in relationship to his humanity. Jesus hands and feet are nailed to the cross and he only has use of his mouth. But oh how he uses his mouth in preaching the greatest sermon that has been ever preached. He takes the cross and makes it his pulpit. He speaks seven words from the cross!

1. The Word of Forgiveness (Luke 23:34)
   Then said Jesus, Father, forgive them; for they

know not what they do. And they parted his rai-
ment, and cast lots.

2. The Word of Salvation (Luke 23:43)
    And Jesus said unto him, Verily I say unto thee,
    today shalt Thou be with me in paradise.

3. The Word of Affection (John 19:26-27)
    When Jesus therefore saw his mother, and the
    disciple by, whom he loved, he saith unto his
    mother, Woman, behold thou son! Then he saith
    to the disciple, Behold thy mother! And from
    that hour that disciple took her unto his own
    home.

4.The Word of Suffering (John 19:28)
    After this, Jesus knowing that all things were
    now accomplished, that the scripture might be
    fulfilled, saith , I thirst.

3. The Word of Anguish (Mark 15:34)
    And at the ninth hour Jesus cried with a loud
    voice, saying, Eloi, Eloi, lama sabachthani? Which
    is, being interpreted, My God, my God, why hast
    thou forsaken me?

4. The Word of Victory (John 19:30)
    When Jesus therefore had received the vinegar,
    he said, It is finished: and he bowed his head,
    and gave up the ghost.

5. The Word of Contentment (Luke 23:46)
    And when Jesus had cried with a loud voice, he

said, Father into thy hands I commend my spirit: and having said thus, he gave up the ghost.

Encouraging Words

Let God fill your mouth with positive words. Learn to give compliments. Learn to give encouraging words. The word "encourage" means to "inspire courage." All of us have areas in which we feel insecure. We lack courage, and that lack of courage often hinders us from accomplishing the positive things that we would like to do. The latent potential within people around you are waiting your encouraging words...Encouragement requires empathy and seeing the world from the other person's perspective, We must learn what is important to the other person. Only then can we give encouragement. With verbal encouragement, we are communicating, "I know. I care. I am with you. How can I help?" We are trying to show that we believe in the other person's abilities. We are giving credit and praise. Most of us have more potential than we ever develop. What holds us back is often courage." [16]

Kind Words

Love is kind. If we are to communicate love, we must use kind words. That has to do with the way we speak. The same sentence can have two different meanings, depending on how you say it...Sometimes our words are saying one thing, but our tone of voice is saying another. We are sending double messages...We can share hurt, pain, and even anger in a kind manner, and that will be an expression of love. ..The manner in which we speak is exceedingly important. An ancient sage once said, "A soft answer turns away anger." [17]

Humble Words

Love makes requests, not demands. ..The way we express our desires, however, is all-important. If the come across as demands, we have erased the possibility of intimacy and we drive people away. If, however, we make known our needs and desires as requests, we are giving guidance, not ultimatums. [18]

Breakthrough-Questions and Answers for Growth

1. Are you conscious and careful with the words that you speak?

_____

_____

_____

_____

_____

_____

2. Do you believe that you have a problem with gossiping and lying?

_____

_____

_____

_____

_____

_____

3. Do you speak with grace seasoned with salt in your relationships?

_____

_____

_____

_____

_____

_____

_____

_____

4. Have you injured someone with words recently?

_____

_____

_____

_____

_____

_____

_____

_____

5. Have anyone injured you with their words recently (explain)?

_____

_____

_____

_____

_____

_____

_____

_____

6. Do you find yourself speaking more negative or posi-tive words (explain)?

_____

_____

_____

_____

_____

_____

_____

_____

7. Are you willing to grow in how you speak words?

_____

_____

_____

_____

_____

_____

_____

_____

8. What good things will you began to speak?

_____

_____

_____

_____

_____

_____

_____

Chapter 6 –
The Renewal Season

In the **season of renewal** God has promised that He will renew your **strength**. After the 150 days of molting a new eagle has emerged. This is a new eagle (new feathers, new beak and his feet is healed). He is stronger and stands as a new eagle upon the top of the mountain and waits for the wind to blow! When he feels the wind is right, he is renewed and he soars through the air! Flies higher! His eyesight is so much better that he flies into the sun. He Soars! That is what the word means in Isaiah 40:31.

> **But they that wait upon the Lord shall renew their strength; they shall mount up with wings like eagles. (Isaiah 40:31).**

The word renew means to begin or take up again, as an acquaintance, a conversation, etc.; to make effective for an additional period; to restore or replenish. The Hebrew word for renew is the word "chalaph" which means to pass on or away, pass through, grow up, change, to show newness. It is just beyond description how God in His infinite wisdom would after so much pain, destruction, and despair that the eagle would experience through the molting stage, would now survive and become a new bird.

Hershel Walker

One of the most inspiring sports that I ever heard is the story of Hershel Walker. College history has recorded him as the greatest running back in collegiate football. His story began in the little town of Riceville, Georgia. As a little boy in school Hershel had a speech impediment that left him with low self-esteem, low self-pride, and a low value of himself. His teacher made him sit in the back of the class. Hershel was also over weight. He walked with his head down because his heart was filled with fear. The kids at his school teased him, bullied him and beat him. These negative experiences were traumatic. It left Hershel with deep emotional wounds, unhealed hurts, resentment and a burning anger.

After one day of a beating from his classmates Hershel made a radical decision. He decided to develop a new Hershel. He decided to take his anger and turn it into a driving force to make him a better person. So for one year Hershel every day did 5,000 set ups and 5000 push- ups. He ran and exercised. Soon a transformation began to take place in Hershel's life. Hershel body took the form of a well- tuned athlete.

He soon began a running regiment where he raced against the train that passed through his town. He also began a training regimen with the school coach and made great strides as a football player. He soon became one of the top high school recruits in the nation playing on both sides of the ball. He broke high school football records. Yet Hershel's plan after high school did not include football. Hershel desired to join the Marines because he wanted to hurt somebody. His heart was filled with rage because of the bulling and pain that he received from the kids at his school.

But destiny would have it that Hershel would accept a scholarship to play football at the University of Georgia in the SEC. In three years he led his team to the National College Football Championship and he won the Heisman Trophy in his junior year. His status on the field soon gain him acclaim and fame around the world. Hershel took his anger and channeled it into a positive fuel of athletic achievement. Just like the eagle he renewed his strength by developing his God given talent into productive energy. His college records still stand today. Hershel Walker became an eagle that soared in the history.

A New You

It's all about a new you! God desires for you to walk now as a new person. Since God is creating a new you, be open now for freshness in your life. Be open to new opportunities. Be open for promotion and increase. God has renewed you for this new season in your life. If you are to be successful you must be open to new ideas. Be willing to reinvent yourself.

The scripture says that God's ways are not our ways and His thoughts are not our thoughts. They are higher and better than our ways. That tells me that God's dream for your life is much more bigger that your own. When a door closes, something doesn't work out, don't sit around in self-pity thinking, Poor old me. No, we may have a reason to feel sorry for ourselves, but we don't have a right. God is still on the throne. If something did not work out the way that you had it planned, let it go and get ready for the new thing that God has for you.

Mary McLeod Bethune

Mary McLeod Bethune was the youngest of seventeen children. She was born in South Carolina, back in the late 1800's to slaves. In spite of all the odds, she got a good education and even went to college. From the time that she was a girl, she desired to go to Africa one day and teach children. She had this dream year after year. She just knew that one day she would be teaching those students. As she neared graduation from College, she sent her application in to a well-known missionary organization. She was a straight A student with an impeccable reputation. You couldn't meet a finer young woman. Week after week she waited she waited, hoping, praying, believing that she would be accepted. But the day came the news she didn't want to hear. For some reason she had been turned down. She was devastated. She said it felt as if something died inside her that day.

Working with children in Africa was what Mary McLeod Bethune wanted to do with her life. But remember when one door closes, if you have faith in God, He will open a new door. Instead of thinking about how bad life had been to her, she developed a new attitude. "If I can't teach the children over there, then I'll teach the students here," she said. Mary Bethune decided to open her own school. She had no money, no building, and no equipment, but where there is a will, there is a way. She found cardboard boxes and used them as desks. She strained red berries so her students could use the juice as ink in their pens. She and her students raised money for their books every week by hauling thousands of pounds of garbage down to the local dump.

Several years went by. A college nearby noticed what was going on and asked Mary's school to join forces. The two schools became Bethune-Cookman College, which is now known as Bethune-Cookman University in Daytona Beach, Florida. Mary Bethune went on to become the first African American woman to be a college president. In 1932, President Franklin Roosevelt appointed her as an advisor to his cabinet, making her the first African American woman to serve as a presidential advisor.

Your renewal season is all about you dreaming a new dream! Put on a new attitude! And like the eagle with its new feathers, new beak, new talons and new eyes: you walk into your new path! God has you in the palm of His hand. He holds victory in your future. The Scripture says in Isaiah 60:1, "Arise and shine, for your light has come."

Ephesians 4:22-24 (AMP) states "Strip yourselves of your former nature-put off and discard your old unrenewed self-which characterized your previous manner of life and becomes corrupt through lust and desires that spring from delusion; And be constantly renewed in the spirit of your mind-having a fresh mental and spiritual attitude; And put on the new nature (the regenerate self) created in God's image, (Godlike) in true righteousness and holiness.

Breakthrough-Questions and Answers for Growth

1. What great expectations do you have in the Lord?

_____

_____

_____

_____

_____

_____

_____

2. What new goals are you working on in your life?

_____

_____

_____

_____

_____

_____

_____

3. What new things is God working in you right now?

_____

_____

_____

_____

_____

_____

_____

_____

4. Are you willing to let go of the old and embrace the new?

_____

_____

_____

_____

_____

_____

_____

_____

Chapter 7 –
Flying with Other Eagles

The story is told of a farmer who found an egg on his chicken farm. He brought the egg home and in a few days the egg hatched. To the farmer's surprise it was a little eaglet. So the chickens and this little eaglet were raised together on the farm. They did everything together. They played together. They ate together. They worked together. They even slept together. But one day the little eaglet looked up and saw a big eagle flying. He looked at this eagle because he had never seen an eagle before. He looked at this eagle's eyes and he looked at his eyes. He looked at this eagle's beak and it looked like his beak. He looked at this eagle's talons and he looked at his talons. He looked at this eagle's wings and he looked at his wings. He thought to himself I must be an eagle.

I Ain't No Chicken

As the eagle circled in the skies above the farm, the eagle shouted from the skies, "Little eaglet, climb up on the hill! Run and jump! Spread your wings and catch the wing and come up and fly with me!" As the little eaglet made up his mind that he would take the challenge; his heart began to pound with excitement, enthusiasm and expectation. The chickens began to cry, "Oh no, you cannot fly because you are not an eagle but you are a chicken." The little eagle shook his head and said, "I ain't no chicken! I am an eagle and God has created me to fly." The eaglet took off running and jumped off the edge of the cliff and flapped his wings and caught a strong current of wind and began to fly! He accomplished what he was created to do because he was an eagle!

The problem is that too many of us flounder as chickens rather than fly as eagles. While eagles soar and scan the skies, chickens are busy looking down and eating off the ground. Yes, they do survive from lower-level consumption, but they don't fly far or do much because they are too busy pecking at the ground below them. They never move beyond lower thinking into the power of spreading their wings like eagles and flying high. Your mission-should you accept it-is to look up and consider who you are and where you're going. Will you choose to eat small kernel thoughts off the ground, or will you seek the mountaintop summits of success with those who overcome the giants of life and rise above the storm? As tasty as chicken may be to those who consume it, always remember that chickens mostly eat waste. Their overhead counterparts are too high to consume what was; eagles only eat what is.

Life is filled with chickens. Especially with their heads looking down, they could be squashed, decapitated, or destroyed. Their vulnerability is that they remain within the reach of the giants of possible destruction. Giants only fight what they can reach. They only find the treasure that lies in low places. So chickens and those who have chicken ideas are always in the reach of those who seek to destroy them.

If you have lived with chickens but thought like an eagle, it is only a matter of time before someone will see the eagle in you and allow you to spread your wings and fly higher. But keep in mind, if you want to go for it as an eagle, you must let go of the chicken's perspective. Don't let the giant problems, budget restrictions, or even legitimate excuses deter your dreams and overpower your passions.

You must start on the ground, but for God's sake end up in the air! From the eagle's view, the giants shrink and become inconsequential. From the eagle's view, new opportunities are always within sight. The eagle sees what lies before him while the chicken's view is only what lies beneath him! Eagles never fear giants because they dwell too high to live at risk! For the closet eagles reading this material, it's time to spread your wings and lift your vision. We are about to sail far beyond our yesterdays into the cerulean celestials of what lies before us. ...It's time to consider what you could attain if you cast off the weight of yesterday and embrace the galling winds of a changed mind and heart.[19]

Whitney Houston

Whitney Houston was an icon to millions around the world. She has been called the "Queen of Pop." Others called her singing, "breathless exhilaration with flashes of musical and emotional lightning." While others said, "her exquisite vocal fluidity and purity of tone...infused a lyric with mesmerizing melodrama." With her bright smile, incredible voice, and acting charisma she was one of the world's bestselling music artists, having sold over 170 million albums, singles and videos worldwide. She was commonly referred to as "The Voice... blessed with astonishing vocal range and extraordinary technical skill, able to connect with a song and drive home its drama and emotion with incredible precision."

Houston was the most awarded female artist of all time, according to Guinness World Records. Indeed she was a rare gift from God to us. Because of Whitney's breakthrough into the music industry, doors were opened for other African-Americans female artists. But yet with all of her success and wealth she struggled in her personal life as all of us struggle with sin. In her interview, appearing on the Oprah Winfrey's season premiere, Whitney admitted on the show to using drugs with former husband Bobby Brown, who "laced marijuana with rock cocaine.' She told Oprah, doing drugs was an everyday thing...I wasn't happy by that point in time, I was losing myself." On February 11, 2012, Houston was found dead in suite 434 at the Beverly Hilton Hotel, submerged in a bathtub. Many people described her personal struggles as, "an eagle running around with chickens."

Association Will Bring Assimilation

There is no doubt that association will bring assimilation. Chickens are those persons in your life that are bringing you down. These are the people that drain your strengthen, sap your creativity and stipend your growth.

They are hindrances and like a leech they can suck everything good that is within you. Chickens are really jealous of your talents and gifts. They want you never ever to be able to rise to your God given abilities as an eagle soaring above your circumstances but rather they want you to remain in the place of mediocrity and average. Chickens are unhealthy, toxic and hateful and if you are not careful they will surround you like vultures on a dead corpse. Every chicken in your life need to be deleted from your phone and eliminated from your life.

Healthy Relationships

There are five kinds of relationships that are necessary to complete your assignment on earth: mentors, protégés, friends, enemies and golden connections. **Mentors** are those who change you. Mentors are teachers of wisdom. Wisdom determines the success of your life. There are two ways to receive wisdom. Your mistakes and mentors are a great factor in the wisdom in your life. Various mentors will enter and exit your life. Mentors are the difference between poverty and prosperity; decrease and increase; loss and gain; pain and pleasure; deterioration and restoration. **Protégés** are those who challenge you. A protégé is an enthusiastic learner. The wisdom of the mentor is perpetuated through the protégé. True success will produce a successor. A protégé is someone who discerns, respects, and pursues the answers God has stored in the mentor for their life. **Friends** are those who comfort you. A best friend loves you the way that you are. Often times your friend is your cheerleader and sees what you do right. But also a true friend will tell you when you are wrong.

Enemies are those who reward you. When God decides to promote you he will send an enemy in your life. An enemy is God's announcement that He is ready to take you to the next level. **Golden Connections** are those who link you. A golden connection is anyone that God uses to connect you to your destiny. [20]

Keys that Strengthen your Relationships

Everything you need or want is hidden in someone near you. God stores His heavenly treasure in earthen vessels. What you respect will move toward you. When you respect someone's gift, your enthusiasm will be apparent. They will respond to you. When God wants to bless you, He places a person in your life. God knows how to staff your weakness. What you don't have, He has placed near you. It is your responsibility to respect and find it. Someone is always observing you who is capable of greatly blessing you. Someone is watching you struggle. Someone knows you're having difficulties. They could help you with your problems...if you would reach out toward them.

Connecting with the Right People

Your destiny is too great to reach on your own. God has already arranged supporters to speak faith into you. He has placed others in your path to inspire you, to challenge you, to help you grow and accomplish your dreams. But some people will never reach their highest potential because they never get away from the wrong people.

Not everyone can go where God is taking you. Connect with those who understand your destiny, friends who appreciate your uniqueness, encouragers who can call forth your seeds of greatness. You do not need those who push you down, tell you what you can't become, and never give their approval even when you do well.

God Will Replace the Negative with the Positive

If you remove the negative people from your life, God will bring positive people into it. Is your inner circle of friends holding you back? Are those closest to you with you but not for you? If you find that it takes constant effort to win their support and encouragement, they likely don't understand your destiny.

The Scripture says, "Do not throw your pearls before swine" (Matthew 7:6 NASB). You could say your pearl is your gift, your personality. It's who you are. When you get around true friends, people who really believe in you, they won't be jealous of your gifts. They won't constantly question who you are. They won't try to talk to you out of your dreams. It will be just the opposite. They'll help you polish your pearl. They'll give you ideas. They'll connect you with people they know. They'll help push you further along.

Do not waste time with people who don't value your gifts or appreciate what you have to offer. That's casting your pearl before swine. Those closest to you should celebrate who you are and be happy when you succeed. They should believe in the very best of you.

If that doesn't describe those in your inner circle, move them out. You can be nice. You can still be friends from a distance. But your time is too valuable to spend with people who are not 100 percent for you. It's not the quantity of friends that's important; it's the quality of friends. I would rather have two good friends who I know are for me 100 percent than have fifty friends who are only for me 80 percent.

Scripture shares the story (see Mark 5:22-24, 35-43) of a man named Jairus who pleaded with Jesus to come to his house where his daughter lay dying and heal her. Jesus and the man were on their way when the word came by messenger: "You don't need to come. She has already died."

But Jesus replied, "Don't worry about it. She'll be okay. We're coming anyway."

Jesus would not let anyone go with Him except Peter, James, and John. They were members of His inner circle. Now, the others with Him were good people too. They loved the Lord. But Jesus said, "I only want these three to go."

Why was that? Jesus knew when He entered the room where the little girl was dead, He needed to be surrounded by true believers who would not question who He was or what He intended to do. Jesus did not need doubters or skeptics asking, "Are you sure you're the Son of God? Have you ever done this before? What if it doesn't work? Do you have a backup plan?"

When you are in the heat of battle and need God's favor, you can't afford to have naysayers and doubters in your inner circle. Jesus did not need to hear things like, "Do you really think she'll get well? My grandmother died of the same thing.

We all need people who are joined in spirit with us and say, "If you're bold enough to believe, count me in. I'm bold enough to agree with you." You need supporters who will come into agreement with you and release their faith, not doubters who tell you what you can't do. When Jesus entered the child's room, all those gathered were distraught and weeping. Don't be upset. She's not dead," Jesus said, "she's only sleeping." Some mourners turned on Jesus, mocking Him.

His response is one of the keys to living a life of victory. Mark 5:40 says, "They laughed and jeered at Him. But Jesus put them all out" (AMP). Jesus showed them the door. His attitude was, "I don't need your doubt."

If you find yourself surrounded by people who mock and doubt you, show them the door just as Jesus did. He didn't allow anyone into the room except the girl's parents and His inner circle. He then spoke to the child and she came back to life. Jesus could have healed her in front of the laughing and mocking crowd. He's the Son of God. He could do anything.

But I believe Jesus wanted to make the point that your inner circle is extremely important. If Jesus took the time to weed out the doubters, surely you and I should be that concerned about our own inner circles....

Iron Sharpens Iron

Proverbs 27:17 says, "As iron sharpens iron, so one person sharpens another" (NIV). Are your friends making you stronger? Are they challenging you to become a better parent, a better spouse, a better co-worker, a better member of your community? You cannot soar with the eagles as long as you're hanging out with the turkeys. So rid yourself of relationships that drain you, drag you down, or leave you feeling the worse for wear.....Your time on this earth is brief and valuable. You have a destiny to fulfill, and you can't make it happen if you are carrying needy and negative people on your back. The solution is found in Mark 5:40. Show them the door. Be kind. Be polite. But pull away....

You may not be aware of the draining effect a negative person is having on you. How much more could you accomplish, grow, and enjoy if you moved out those who are with you but not for you? Make sure the people in your inner circle believe in you. They should celebrate your gifts and push you ahead, not hold you back.

I can't think of anything worse than to come to the end of life and realize that someone you trusted kept you from becoming the person God created you to be. You may be fearful of losing a friend and being lonely, but you never give up something for God that He doesn't make up for by giving you something better in return.

If you'll make the change, God will not only give you new friends, He will give you better friends. Friends about whom you don't have to wonder, Are they for me are against me? Friends who don't try to manipulate you into who they want you to be, but rather they celebrate you and help you become who God created you to be. [21]

Breakthrough-Questions and Answers for Growth

1. If you did a present assessment of the people in your life, how can they be described?

   _____

   _____

   _____

   _____

   _____

   _____

   _____

2. Can you describe the present mentor or mentors in your life?

   _____

   _____

   _____

   _____

   _____

   _____

   _____

3. Do you have any chickens in your life that needs to be deleted?

_____

_____

_____

_____

_____

_____

_____

_____

4. Have you decided to run with other eagles (explain)?

_____

_____

_____

_____

_____

_____

_____

_____

5. What have you decided that you will do to foster more
   healthy and productive relationships in your life?

   _____

   _____

   _____

   _____

   _____

   _____

   _____

   _____

   _____

   _____

   _____

   _____

Chapter 8 –
Soaring, Running and
Walking in Victory

LeBron James was crowned with his first NBA Championship during the 2011-12 Season. After nine frustrating seasons, he hoisted up the shining gold Championship Trophy on his home court in Miami. After a painful departure from his home state basketball team the Cleveland Cavaliers and after his controversial signing with the Miami Heat; LeBron joined forces with superstars DeWayne Wade and Chris Bosh. It seemed like everything was in order for them to take the crown in the 2010-11 Championship series but they suffered an embarrassing, humiliating, and crushing loss to the Dallas Mavericks. The vicious criticism, negativity and pressure that were levied against this man were amazing.

But in the 2011-2012 season championship finals it seemed that there was a new LeBron. His fire, passion, poise, persistency, precision and power were just too much for the young Oklahoma City Thunder team. His three point shot in the closing moments of game four after he was carried off the court with leg cramps and re-entered the game while lipping on one leg, will go down in NBA legend forks ore as one the outstanding displays of gritty determination. After the victory the sport analyst asked the smiling and jubilant LeBron, "What made the difference this year?" LeBron responded, "I matured and I humbled myself after that loss." LeBron renewed his self, skill set and soared to new heights as a person and a basketball player.

Soaring never just happens. It is the result as we have learned of strong mental effort-thinking clearly, courageously and confidently. The bible says, "They shall mount up with wings like an eagle. They shall run and not be weary and they shall walk and not faint." They shall not become weary! Walk and not faint! The eagle now is able to fly into the direction of the sun. Thank God for renewal! Isn't it interesting that the procession is fly, run and walk. God does not only give the eagle new feathers, but the eagle now has new feet (claws) and a new beak. It is amazing what God is able to do in the life and power of renewal. The Apostle Paul shares with believers that there is new power that every believer is to walk in.

Ephesians 1: 19-23, "And what is the exceeding greatness of his power to us-ward who believe, according to the working of his mighty power, which he wrought in Christ, when he raised him from the dead, and set him at his own right hand in the heavenly places, far above all principality, and power, and might, and dominion, and every name that is named, not only in this world, but also in that which is to come: and hath put all things under his feet, and gave him to be the head over all things to the church, which is his body, the fullness of him that filleth all in all.

Soaring, Running, Walking
Above, Around and Through Stuff

God said that you will be able to soar, run and walk like the eagle. Isaiah says it like this, "But they that wait upon the Lord shall renew their strength: they shall mount up with wings as eagles: they shall run, and not be weary; and they shall walk and not faint." In any normal human development and progression one always first walks, runs and then soars. But in this progression the word talks about soaring, running and then walking. I believe that God is saying that in any circumstance that He will give you the power to overcome. It is in the overcoming of obstacles that you ready experience spiritual grow and development. It is the stuff that you have to go through that truly shapes character. Character is shaped in the trails of life.

Jimmy R. Stevens

The 2012 Olympic Games

In the 2012 Olympic Games in London, England we were treated with a spectacular opening ceremony and competition. The opening show mesmerized us from the awesome lights shows, music entertainment by legendary Paul McCarthy and even the Queen and James Bond teamed up. The parade of 204 nations marched into the stadium by the thousands of screaming fans as millions watched around the world. During the two weeks many sport fans watched the performances of the athletes like American gymnast, Babby Douglas, American swimmer, Micheal Phelps and Jamaican sprinter, Usain Holt only to mention a few.

But perhaps the most inspiring performance for me was a South African man who ran with no legs. He was a paraplegic. A paraplegic is one who has to use paretic for legs. As he ran around the track with some of the fastest runners in the world my heart leaped with excitement. At first I wanted to feel sadness for him. But why should I feel sorry for a soaring eagle. There was a heated argument that persisted that he should never be allowed to run with able bodied men. The argument was that he could never win. Why should he run? But he was allowed to run. I so glad that he ran because he proved to a septic world than he was an eagle. Can you just imagine what stuff he has endured all of his life. Can you imagine the negativity and harsh criticisms that he has endured. But in London, England he shined like a bright light in a dark world. With his prosthetic legs he soared, ran and walked his way into Olympic quarter finals in the history. Although he did not win a metal he won the admiration of millions around the world. True courage and determination cannot always be measured by a first, second or third place finish. Jesus taught us that the "Race is not given to the swift or the strong but he that endures to the end."

Walk in Victory

You are called to walk in victory. Many of the persons that God used in the bible had something that they had to overcome and walk in victory. It was not that they did not have flaws and failures but it was that they possessed a great faith in God. It was their faith in God that gave them the victory. These men and women are called the "Heroes of Faith."

- Hebrews 11:39, "All of these obtained a good report through faith"...

- I John 5:4, "For whatsoever is born of God over-cometh the world: and this is the victory that overcometh the world, even our faith."

- Abraham overcame physical limitations at the age of ninety-nine to father his son Isaac, the son of promise

- Moses overcame a speech impediment to become a great spokesman for the Lord and his people

- Sarah overcame barrenness to become the mother of a nation

- Rahab overcame the past of prostitution to become the great grandmother of King David

- King David overcame a murder of a loyal soldier by seeking the forgiveness and cleansing of God

- Gideon overcame a deep sense of inadequacy to become a mighty man of valor

- Jephthah overcame a life as a gang leader and destructive behavior to become a judge in Israel

- Samson overcame a serious moral fall to destroy more of his enemies in death than in life

- Esau overcame the anger and resentment in his heart after being tricked by his brother Jacob

- Jacob overcame a life time of scheming and trickery to trusting in God to provide for his needs

Breakthrough-Questions and Answers for Growth

1. What do you believe that God is calling you to soar over?

_____

_____

_____

_____

_____

_____

_____

2. What do you believe that God is calling you to run with?

_____

_____

_____

_____

_____

_____

_____

3. What things do you believe that God is calling you to walk through?

_____

_____

_____

_____

_____

_____

_____

4. How have you been renewed in your mind and heart concerning your journey as you have studied this word?

_____

_____

_____

_____

_____

_____

_____

5. Have you embraced the truth that you are a Christian eagle who can soar?

_____

_____

_____

_____

_____

_____

_____

_____

_____

_____

_____

_____

Chapter Nine –
Buckle Up For You're Riding
on God's Eagle Wings

The President of the United States travels on the airplane "Airforce One". Airforce One is a tremendous aircraft uniquely equipped with every amenity imaginable to insure the president's safety, communication and comfort. It costs $179,750.00 per hour to operate this jet. Airforce One is called the flying White House because of its awesome amenities which include 4,000 feet of floor space. It is six stories high, the plane is 231 feet 10 inches long with a wing span of 195 feet and 8 inches, able to travel at the speed of 630 miles per hour, near supersonic speed.

This aircraft is equipped with an executive suite for the commander-in-chief; it functions as a mobile command center in the event of an attack on the United States. Also it can function as an operating room with a doctor permanently on board! The plane has two food preparation galleys able to serve 100 people at a time. Defenses include infrared missile, radar jamming technology and a host of top secret aerial defenses electronic counter measures. Several cargo planes travel ahead to provide services in remote locations. Airforce One can refuel in mid-air with unlimited range.

Other amenities include fax and copy machines, broad band satellite radar, dozens of phone lines, and high speed internet. This jet has a total of seventy seats with twenty-six crew members that are on board at all times which include senior advisors, secret service officers, traveling press and other guest. It is the pilot's job on "Airforce One" to make sure that the leader of the free world gets to one destination to the other destination.

Traveling on the Wings of God

But as believers we travel and journey on something that is more awesome than the Airforce One Jet, Continental, Southwest, Delta, Boeing 747, or a Gemini Private Jet. We as believers actually journey on the blush Wings of the Almighty God. God desires to take us from one destination to the next destination in life and serve us with His loving care and protection. In the fifteen chapter of the book of Exodus the children of Israel are in the third month of their emancipation from Egyptian slavery. The Almighty God speaks to His servant leader Moses and says, "Thus you shall say to the house of Jacob, and tell the children of Israel: You have seen what I did to the Egyptians and how I bore you on eagles' wings and brought you to myself." God wanted the children of Israel to know that it was Him that had brought them out. God also wants you to know that it was Him that brought you and that will bring you into you destiny. God likens Himself to the Mother Eagle.

When the little eaglet is learning how to fly the first thing he does is jump out of the nest. While the little eaglet is flapping, fluttering and falling through the air the Mother Eagle swoops down and comes to the rescue. Before the little eaglet crashes to the earth the eaglet is saved by the Mother Eagle's wings, the eaglet rides on the wings to safety.

God wants you to never forget that He is the one who bares you on His Eagle's wings! God was the one who carried you through sickness, surgery, suffering, financial strain, stress, anxiety, bankruptcy, grief, depression! Just like the little eaglet you have been riding all along on God's wings of protection and provision. There were three principles that God wanted the children of Israel to learn about His eagle wings.

Escape the World

God also wanted them to know that their deliverance was due to His Hand. In Exodus 19:4 God said, "You seen what I did to the Egyptians..." Egypt is always symbolic of the world. We live and we must understand that there are two systems. There is a world system and there is a kingdom system. One system is ruled and governed by Satan and the other system is ruled and governed by God. God's people had been in slavery for four hundred years but God had delivered them out. We really have three enemies that we fight each day; the world, Satan and the flesh.

Ephesians 2:2-3, "You once walked according to the course of world, according to the prince of the power of the air, the spirit who now works in the sons of disobedience, among whom also we all once conducted ourselves in the lusts of our flesh, fulfilling the desires of the flesh and of the mind, and were by nature children of wrath, just as the others. (NKJV)

There was a time that you were once governed by the world, Satan and the flesh. Every decision that you made was according to these three powers.

"Satan is called both "the god of this world" 2 Corinthians 4:4, "whose minds the god of this world has blinded, who do not believe, lest the light of the gospel of the glory of Christ, who is the image of God, should shine on them" and the "prince of this world" John 12:31, "Now is the judgment of this world, now the prince of this world will be cast out." This word world (cosmos) is used 185 times in the New Testament. Basically the word denotes an ornament or order. But usually the New Testament views the world (cosmos) as an orderly system that functions apart from God. Satan's aim is to create a system that rivals God's kingdom but that leaves Him out. It is to promote a counterfeit order. Basically, the world is evil because it is independent of God. It may contain good aspects as well as overtly evil aspects, but its inherent evil lies in its being independent of God and rival to Him. This sharp rivalry surfaces in such verses as James 1:27, where the believer is told to keep himself unstained from the world; in 4:4, where friendship with the world is said to be hostility toward God; and in 1 John 2:18, where John declares that all that is in the world is not from the Father." [22]

> **James 1:27, "Pure and undefiled religion before God and the Father is this: to visit orphans and widows in their trouble, and to keep oneself unspotted from the world." (NKJV)**

> **James 4:4, "Adulterers and adulteresses! Do you not know that friendship with the world is enmity with God? Whosoever therefore wants to be friend of the world makes himself an enemy with God. (NKJV)**

> **I John 2:15-17, "Do not love the world or the things in the world. If anyone loves the world, the love of the Father is not in him. For all that is in the world-the lust of the flesh, the lust of the eyes, and the pride of life-is not of the Father but is of the world. And the world is passing away, and the lust of it: but he who does the will of God abides forever." (NKJV)**

"To achieve his aim, Satan must try to make the values of his godless system seem attractive. Thus he works to make people give top priority to self as number one and to the here and now as most important.... In 1 John 2:16, the emphasis is on self as number one. Satisfy the lusts of the flesh, Satan counsels. Try to get what the inordinate desires of the eyes make you covet. And build a self-sufficient, arrogant attitude that arises from boasting about possessions one has in life. This selfishness is of course, the prevailing philosophy of the world, and it comes from Satan who promoted himself from the beginning. Satan also seeks to focus people's attention on the present rather than on eternity. That is why John reminds us in 1 John 2:17 that the world passes away but the one that does the will of God abides forever. Thus Satan seeks to achieve his purposes by trying to change our priorities (self-first) and our perspective (here and now more important). In reality the truth is that God is first and eternity most important." [23]

The Christian and the World

You are to separate from the world. Pure religion, James wrote, is to keep oneself unstained from the world (James 1:27). The same word "unstained" or "unspotted" is used of Christ in I Peter 1:19. Thus the believer's separation from the world means Christ likeness in this world. This includes having His perspectives, His standards, His goal (to do the will of the Father).... But of course, the believer, though separated from the world, has to live his life in the world. Thus we have to have contact with evil things and evil people. The only way to avoid such contact would be to "go out of the world" (I Cor. 5:10). Such separation by suicide" Paul did not recommend. How, then can we be properly related to the world in which we are situated? Here are two guidelines. (1). Use it but do not abuse it (I Cor. 7:31). (2). Enjoy but do not love the things of the world (I Timothy 6:17; I John 2:15). What God gives us in this world we can legitimately enjoy, as long as we realize that all things are uncertain and that our dependence is on God whether He gives us little or much (Phil. 4:12; I Tim. 6:17)...The believer can live victoriously in Satan's world through faith in Christ who Himself has become the victor over Satan (I John 5:4-5). No contingency is attached to the promise in these verses. Every believer, whether new or mature, has victory simply because he is a believer. Effecting that victory, will involve habits, defenses, activities, but it is our faith in Jesus that makes us believers and thus overcomers, sufficient to live Christ like lives in the satanic world. [24]

Armor Bearers and Pallbearers

God desires to deliver you out of bondage and put you into the Kingdom of God. I once heard Evangelist Tellis Chatman of Detroit, Michigan said, "There is a difference between an armor bearer and a pallbearer." An armor bearer is anyone who shares the load with you of life. They are willing to assist you as you carry out your goals and objectives. But a pallbearer is anyone who is helping to carry you to the graveyard. These persons are not waiting until you die but while you are living these persons who enable you in toxic and unhealthy behavior are those who are bringing you to an early grave. Those who sin with you and help you to sin are carrying you to an early death. Those who encourage you and help ensnare you in different kinds of addictions are pallbearers.

Michael Jackson and Dr. Conrad Murry
While the whole world watched with anticipation of holding someone other than the icon they lost responsible, Michael Jackson's doctor, cardiologist Conrad Murry, was recently found guilty of manslaughter in the untimely death of his most famous patient. Amid the dramatic

evidence presented at the trial, the media had scrutinized every nuance, preference, and possibility of the doctor's actions and motives, all against the backdrop of the tragic death of one of the world's greatest musical superstars.

Every doctor takes the Hippocratic oath as part of their certification to be a licenses physician. The vow includes "the promise to do no harm." It seems clear from the various testimonies and pieces of evidence that Dr. Murry never intended for MJ, or any of his patients for that matter, to die as a result of his treatment.

We know that the esteemed cardiologist did not wake up that fateful morning and say, "I'm going to kill Michael Jackson today." However, the guilty verdict delivered in the trail sends a message that Dr. Murry, despite his good intentions, must be held responsible for his patient's overdose. [25]

It is so easy becoming a victim of a pallbearer even when at times their intention was to be an armor bearer. Your associations and relationships definitely will have a positive or negative impact on your life. So Jesus wants to touch you and get you to jump out of your casket and dismiss those pallbearers and help you find healthy armor bearers on your journey of life. Slavery is always about bondage and emancipation is always about liberation. God is still saying, "I want you out of Egypt (the world system)."

You Will Experience the Wilderness

It is very interesting that the children of Israel had seven experiences in the wilderness on their way to the promised land. Each experience was mandatory for their spiritual growth and development as a people.

Our wilderness experience is also mandatory as we are developing into the stature and fullness of Jesus Christ. God allows us to ride through these experiences to grow us.

First Experience

The first experience in the wilderness was **worship**. In Exodus 15:21 the children of Israel praised God after God brought them through the Red Sea. They sang a song of triumph. For God had triumphal gloriously delivered them through the waters of the Red Sea. God is teaching you to worship Him. Always look to Him and magnify Him for His goodness, truthfulness, faithfulness, grace, justice and mercy. Get your shout on and praise God!

> **Exodus 15:1-3, 21, "Then Moses and the children of Israel sang this song to the Lord, and spoke, saying, "I will sing to the Lord, for He has triumphed gloriously! The horse and its rider He has thrown into the sea! The Lord is my strengthen and song, And He has become my salvation; He is my God, and I will praise Him; My Father's God, and I will exalt Him. The Lord is a man of war; The Lord is His name. And Miriam answered them; Sing to the Lord, For He has triumphed gloriously! The horse and his rider He has thrown into the Sea." (NKJV)**

The Second Experience

The second experience of the children of Israel in the **wilderness** was bitterness. In Exodus 15:22-25 after they worshipped God, God led them to a place called Marah, where the waters were bitter. There are times that God leads us to bitter experiences. The experience is never designed to make us bitter but rather to teach us how to depend on God. God showed Moses a tree. Something that was insignificant. But many times God will use insignificance experiences so that He can bring about our miracle. When this tree was thrown into the waters, the waters became sweet. God is teaching us how to make lemonade!

God is willing to help turn your bitter experience to sweet.

The Third Experience

The third experience of the children of Israel was that they were called to continue to move forward on their journey. They came next to a place called "Elim" where there were seventy palm trees and twelve wells of water. God led them to an oasis in the desert. God will lead you to a place of rest, and relaxation. Sometimes the pace of life is frantic, stressful and demanding. If we don' stop long enough and smell the roses we will come apart emotionally. These palm trees were provided for rest and beauty. Many times the beauty of nature is just the relaxation that we need as we get in touch with the God of nature.

On my last vacation I was completely drained, frustrated and needed rest. It was amazing what I boat ride on the Mississippi River did for me. The breeze of fresh air and the invigorating water refreshed my soul. This week of rest, fine food, soft music, new sights recharged my spiritual battery. These children of Israel got the chance to drink from streams of fresh water and sit under the palm trees in the midst of the hot wilderness.

The Fourth Experience

The fourth experience is recorded in Exodus 16:1-6 where the children of Israel traveled to the Wilderness of Sin. They have now traveled for two months (the fifteenth day of the second month after departing out of the land of Egypt). Here the whole congregation complained and murmured against Moses and Aaron. They complained because now they wished that they had died in Egypt.

> **"Would to God we had died by the hand of the Lord in the land of Egypt, when we sat by the flesh pots, and when we did eat bread to the full; for ye have brought us forth into this wilderness, to kill the whole assembly with hunger." (Exodus 16:2-3)**

They panicked and did not practice trust in God. They developed a complaining spirit. When you just criticize you will walk round with a chronic case of the complaint. A complaining spirit is never trust in God.

The Fifth Experience

Their fifth experience was the provision of God. In Exodus 16:4-36 God will rain down bread from heaven every day for six days (on the six day there was double rained down). They would rest on the Sabbath day to teach them to set that day aside for worship and rest. They were not to stack up the bread for many days. But they were to go out every day and receive the manna from heaven. God is the God of our daily provision.

The Sixth Experience

They now come to Rephidim in Exodus 17:1-7. But here at Rephidim there is no water for the people to drink. The people thirst and complain. The people desire to stone Moses. But here in Rephidim God would provide water out of a rock. God provides out of hard places. God provides out of rocky places.

The Seventh Experience

In this experience the children of Israel is attacked by Amalek. They would have to battle. Moses their leader would go up to the top of the hill and hold up his hands. As he would hold up his hands Israel in the valley would prevail. But his hands got tired and when he would let them down then Amalek in the valley would prevail. But Aaron and Hur held up Moses hands.

And the children of Israel won the battle. And Moses built an altar there and named it Jehovah-Nissi. Because the children of Israel worked together in harmony they won the battle.

You Can Encounter God's Destiny

You will encounter God's destiny. God said, "I bore you on Eagle's wings and brought you. God is bringing you somewhere. Sometimes the enemy tricks us in thinking only about location rather than relationship. God was bringing them to Himself. I bore you on Eagles wings and brought you to myself. It's all about a deeper relationship with God. Until you realize that God is your source.

"Ye have seen what I did unto the Egyptians, and how I bare you on eagle's wings, and brought you unto myself. Now therefore, if ye will obey my voice indeed, and keep my covenant, then ye shall be a peculiar treasure unto me above all people: for all the earth is mine: And ye shall be unto me a kingdom of priests, and an holy nation..." (Exodus 19:4-6)

In Exodus 19 and verses 4-6, there are eight personal pronouns that are used. God brags on Himself.

God said, "What I did to the Egyptians..."

God said, "How I bare you on eagles' wings..."

God said, "And brought you to Myself..."

God said, "If you will obey my voice...

God said, "And keep my covenant..."

God said, "Ye shall be a treasure unto me above all people..."

God said, "The earth is mine..."

God said, "And ye shall be unto me a kingdom of priests and an holy nation..."

Obedience

God demands that the children of Israel be obedient. God demands that you to obedient to His word. There is relationship between love and obedience. Jesus said, "If you love Me, keep My commandments. The one who doesn't love Me will not keep My words" (John 14:15, 24).

- Obedience is the outward expression of your love for God.
- The reward for obedience is that God will make Himself known to you.
- If you have an obedience problem, you have a love problem.
- If you love Him, you will obey Him!

Jesus said, "For whosoever does the will of My Father in heaven, that person is My brother and sister and mother" (Matthew 12:50). Jesus made it clear that obedience is the outflow of our love relationship with God (see John 14:15-21).

James in his letter to believers, emphasized that faith without active obedience is dead-useless. When the disciples obeyed Jesus, they saw and experienced God's mighty power working in and around them. When they did not act in faith, they did not experience His mighty work.

"Even so faith, if it have not works, is dead, being alone. Yea, a man may say, Thou has faith, and I have works: shew me thy faith without thy works, and I will shew thee my faith by my works." (James 2:17-18)

Servants of God do what He directs. They obey. The servant does not have the option of deciding whether or not to obey. Choosing not to do what God commands is rebellion, and such disobedience has consequences.

People are naturally self-centered; we want to please ourselves.... In the process of experiencing God, obedience is your moment of truth. Your obedience (or lack of it) will:

1. Reveal what you believe about God;
2. Determine whether you will come to know Him more intimately;
3. Determine whether you will experience His mighty work in and through you.

You obey because you trust You trust Him because you love Him...Because you know God loves you, you should never question a directive from Him. It will always be right and best. When He expresses His will, you are just to observe, discuss, or debate it. You are not called to "wrestle with it" as many do. You are to obey... Obedience, has its costs. You cannot know and do the will of God without paying the price of adjustment. Counting the cost to follow God's will is one of the major adjustments that you will have to make... Although obedience is costly, it always worth the price. Whenever you think the cost may be too great, consider what it will cost you not to do the will of God...God blesses those who are obedient to Him. The benefits of obedience are beyond our imagination. Obedience brings great blessings. [26]

Three Blessings of Obedience

There are three blessings in particular that God mentions in the scripture in Exodus 19:4-6.

Blessing One

God desires that His people be a peculiar treasure. Have you ever seen a treasure with all the fine jewels and gems? They are not only beautiful with their many colors and brilliance but they are also valuable. You are so valuable to

God. You are His special treasure. You are more valuable than all the diamonds in Africa.

Blessing Two

God desires that you be a King unto him. Not just a king but a kingdom of priests. It was the priest's job to offer sacrifices unto God. When you offer sacrifices also a king reigns over a kingdom. God has desired that you reign and have dominion over his creation.

Blessing Three

God desires that you be a holy nation. You are set apart and sanctified unto Him. As His people He desires that He care and manage the lives of His people. Be always willing to let God care and give direction to your life.

Final Destination

Buckle up and let God carry you on His wings. Recently on the way back from the island of Dominica of the West Indies where a dedicated team of missionaries from our Baptist National and State Convention arrived at the airport in Melville. It had been a great week of ministry of us. We had taken with us a medical doctor and several nurses, VBC teachers, deacons and ministers. We had poured out our talents and love to the people on the island through ministry. We had enjoyed the Caribbean food, warm fellowship and the inspiring word of God. Some of us had refreshed old relationships and those of us traveling for the first time to the island had made new friends. We had worshipped and worked together. Even some of us had a little time to view the beautiful sights, and sounds of other villages on the island. But now it was time for us to go back home to our friends and family in the United States. As I made my way up to the desk in Melville, Dominica to present my passport and my luggage to the attendant, she asked me, "What is your final destination?" I replied "To New Orleans, Louisiana." That day I boarded three different American Airline planes on the way back home. But I realized that Louisiana is not my final destination. But my final destination is Heaven. As you board on the wings of God daily, always be reminded that He desires to carry us from one destination to the next destination. But one day He desires to carry us all the way to our home with Him. In the meantime get busy developing your eagle mentality and experiencing the great wonder of God's work in His world. The world is waiting on you!

Breakthrough-Questions and Answers for Growth

1. Are there any areas in your life where you are struggling with being delivered from the world's system? (Explain)

_____

_____

_____

_____

_____

_____

_____

2. Are there any pallbearers in your life that are hindering your growth? (Explain)

_____

_____

_____

_____

_____

_____

_____

3. Is there anyone presently in your life that is a pall-bearer? (Explain)

_____

_____

_____

_____

_____

_____

_____

4. What was the last wilderness experience that you encountered?

_____

_____

_____

_____

_____

_____

_____

_____

5. What area or areas of disobedience are you struggling with? (Explain)

_____

_____

_____

_____

_____

_____

_____

_____

6. Do you really feel that you are a special treasure?

_____

_____

_____

_____

_____

_____

_____

7. How do you know that you have grown in a deeper and more intimate relationship with God? (Explain)

_____

_____

_____

_____

_____

_____

_____

_____

_____

_____

_____

_____

Bibliography

Chapter One

1. Charles R. Swindoll, Living Above The Level Of Mediocrity (Word Publishing, 1987) pages 48-49
2. Dr. I. V. Hillard, Mental Toughness for Success (Light Publications Houston, Texas 2003), pages 67-68
3. Charles R. Swindoll, Living Above The Level Of Mediocrity (Word Publishing, 1987) pages 19-21
4. Ibid, pages 21-26
5. T.W. Hunt, The Mind Of Christ (Broadman and Holman Publishers, Nashville, Tennessee 1995) pages 4, 6, 9, 13-14

Chapter Two

6. Tony Evans, Our God Is Awesome (Renaissance Productions (Moody Press, Chicago, 1994), pages 37-38.
7. Ibid., (45-47)
8. Matthew Henry Commentary
9. Ibid.,

10. Ibid.,

11. Tony Evans, Our God is Awesome (Renaissance Productions: Moody Press, Chicago, 1994), pages 125-128

Chapter Three

12. Charles R. Swindoll, Living Above The Level of Mediocrity (Word Publishing, 1987), pages 256-257

13. T.W. Hunt, The Mind of Christ (Broadman and Holman Publishers, Nashville, Tennessee 1995) pages 4-5

Chapter Five

14. Gary Chapman, The Five Love Languages (Northfield Publishing, Chicago, 1992) pages 39

15. Harold Ivan Smith, A Time For Healing (Life Way Press, Nashville, Tennessee 1994) page 66

16. Gary Chapman, The Five Love Languages (Northfield Publishing, Chicago, 1992) pages 42, 44

17. Ibid, page 45

18. Ibid, page 48

Chapter Seven

19. T. D. Jakes, Let It Go: Forgive So You Can Be Forgiven, (Atria Books, New York, NY 2012) pages 25-26

20. Mike Murdock, The Law of Recognition (Wisdom International, Denton, Texas 1999) pages 122-123, 201.

21. Joel Osteen, Every Day A Friday, (Faith Books, New York, NY, 2011) pages 135-139

Chapter Nine
22. Charles C. Ryrie, Basic Theology (Moody Publishers, Chicago, 1999) pages 172-174.
23. Ibid., pages 173-174.
24. Ibid., pages 174-176.
25. T.D. Jakes, Let It Go, Forgive So You Can Be Forgiven (Atria Books, New York, NY, 2012) pages 151-152
26. Henry & Richard Blackaby and Claude King (B&H Publishing
27. Group) Nashville, Tennessee 2008) pages 240-244

About the Author

Jimmy Stevens is married to Patricia Stevens. He is the pastor of the New Covenant Faith Baptist Church in Lake Charles, Louisiana. He has a Bachelor of Arts degree in Speech Communications from McNeese State University. His post graduate studies include: New Orleans Baptist Seminary and Cornerstone University. He desires that believers in Christ be trained and equipped for the harvest of souls into the Kingdom.